Bastard-in-Chief

FANCY ROBERTS

Contents

This one is for me.
And everyone else who forgot they were important.
We are.

One

SOPHIE

THE SCENT OF FRESH tortillas hits my nose the moment I follow my best friend through the door of our favorite downtown restaurant. "But what about Emma?"

"Sophie Alexander, it's your thirty-fucking-fifth birthday. You got your divorce papers yesterday. We are going out to get plastered on lethal margaritas tonight to celebrate your freedom from Teeny Peeny *and* you reaching your sexual prime. I already texted Emma, she's spending the night at Bella's house." She shakes her head at me before I can protest, her chin-length hair swinging. "And no, she didn't want to come, I already asked. No normal fifteen-year-old wants to hang out with her mom on a Friday night."

"Happy Birthday, Sophie!" A large table of women greets us as we make our way deeper into the restaurant from the bar. Jess raises her glass in a toast, her margarita already half drunk.

Lauren pushes me into the booth with Jess and a few other ladies from work. I don't know most of them, but I smile anyway. Angela from Marketing slides a margarita to me with a birthday greeting. I take a sip that burns on the way down, as lethal as advertised.

I join in the meaningless chatter while I drink, letting the tequila warm me from the inside. One of the girls from accounting is in the middle of a story about her latest blind date when Jess squeaks, clutching at my arm.

"Oh. My. God." Her nails dig painfully into my upper arm. "Is that Theodore-fuck-me-Sutton?"

"What?" I crane my neck to catch a glimpse. Shit. There he is. The quintessential grumpy boss we all work for is leaning on the bar, sipping from a glass of golden liquid. I'm pretty sure the whole table sighs out loud watching his Adam's apple bob as he swallows.

Everyone in the office is terrified of him, but that doesn't mean he isn't the subject of more than one secret fantasy.

Like the novel I've been writing.

The one that features a hero with dark looks like his, and a gruff exterior.

"Soph!" Lauren snaps a finger in front of my face. "Time for presents!" She shoves a hot pink gift bag into my hands.

"Thanks, babe." I move to tuck the bag under my chair, next to my purse, but Lauren grabs it.

"Nope, you have to open it now. I need to see your face!" She grins at me, the same grin that got us into trouble on more than one occasion in college.

"Lauren..." I give her a warning look before reaching in and pulling out a pink envelope. "Pink? Really?"

Lauren just laughs. "It's a theme. Open it already!"

I take my time reading the card to annoy her, smiling at her use of the nicknames we gave each other back in college.

Bitch,

Have I told you lately how proud of you I am? You already know how I feel about Jake and his actions, but I am so excited to see you finally putting yourself first.

Here's a little something so you can keep pursuing the things that you love, and so you can take care of yourself. Love you!

- Slut

"Aww, thanks babe." Laughing, I wipe my eyes before pulling the first tissue-wrapped shape out of the bag. "Hmm, this feels like a book. Always a good choice." Ripping off the paper reveals a stack of three books—Lucy Score's newest, a signed copy of one of Annette Marie's *Demonized* books for my collection, and a craft book called *Romancing the Beat*.

"So you can finally finish that book instead of spending all your free time writing boring articles for me." Lauren grins at me. "You know I'm dying to read more. You left me hanging at chapter six and I neeeeeeeed to know if they fuck."

She's not wrong. Answering the phones and directing traffic at Mailbox, Inc is just one of the jobs I do to pay the bills. What no one besides Lauren knows, is that I write articles for the company blog under a pen name for extra money.

When Mr. Sutton instructed Lauren to add a blog to Mailbox's website, posting articles about business and technology in order to increase Mailbox's visibility, she was able to hire "Elinor Price" without fuss. Lauren's also the only person who knows that there's a series of unfinished romance novels burning a hole in the hard drive of my laptop at home.

Jake, my ex-husband, hated my love of romances. It should have been a sign.

"These are amazing, thank you." I give her a sideways hug.

"Oh, that's just the start. That was your official birthday gift. Now you have to open your 'Happy Divorce' gift."

"Is it decent for the public? Your face is twitching."

Lauren laughs, taking another long sip of her margarita. "Probably not, but open it anyway. We never got to have a bachelorette party for you since you were already pregnant with Emma and your courthouse wedding didn't let me celebrate my bestie the way she deserves."

Needing to steel myself for whatever it is she's wrapped in here, I take a long draw on my drink for some tequila courage. The weight of the bag gives me no clue what it could be. "I love you and I hate you."

"Hate-love you too, Soph." She winks. "Quit stalling and open the damn gift."

I pull out the first package, stripping the tissue paper from it before Lauren can say anything else. "Lipstick?" I hold up the tube to examine it in the dim light of the restaurant. The black case looks expensive, though I don't recognize the gold "KB" stamped on it. It's a good gift, I never buy myself expensive makeup.

"Nope." Lauren grins. "Take off the cap."

I pull the cap off to reveal a hot pink silicone tip. "Oh my God…is that?" I slam the cap back on, my cheeks burning. "Lauren!" I hiss. "Is that a fucking *vibrator*?"

"That's not even the best part." Lauren is in hysterics. "Open the next one." She grabs at the bag, intending to pull it out for me.

"Is it a dildo? Tell me it's not a fucking dildo, Lauren. I am *not* opening a dildo in public." I glance around wildly catching Mr. Sutton still at the bar. Is he waiting for someone? "Especially where our *boss* could see it."

"Don't be a party pooper, he's not even paying attention to us. Like Theodore Sutton would ever deign to pay attention to the peons. He's probably just waiting for a to-go order."

Nervous, I unwrap the second gift. It's small and square so at least I know I'm not about to end up waving a giant penis in the air. Pulling off the paper reveals a black jewelry box. I crack open the lid. Inside is a gold ring, one of those big statement ones, the quartz-crystal shaped top bold and exciting. Too bad I'm not bold or exciting enough to pull it off.

"Wow. Thanks, Lauren. It's gorgeous." It is, it really is, I'm just not cool enough to wear it myself. I pull it out of the box and slip it on the middle finger of my right hand, the ring long enough to cover my entire knuckle. This is the kind of thing Lauren would wear to work. The only ring I've ever worn was my wedding ring, the plain silver band all Jake and I could afford when we got married at twenty. He never bought me anything else—not that we would have had the money for it even if he'd bothered.

The weight of it on my right hand is as unfamiliar as the emptiness of my left ring finger. The more I stare at it, the more I'm convinced I've seen her wearing this exact ring. "Isn't this almost exactly like the one you have?"

A mischievous grin sneaks across Lauren's face. "It's *exactly* like the one I have. It has a secret." She pulls my hand toward her and slips the ring off my finger. "See this little circle?" She points to a button I hadn't noticed on the underside of the decorative shape. "Tap it."

I do, shrieking and nearly dropping it when the whole thing starts buzzing in the palm of my hand. Jess and the other girls at the table demand to see so it gets passed around, while I take a deep breath and try not to throttle my best friend. She took me and Emma in when I left Jake, I can't kill her over a vibrator ring.

Shit. Is Sutton still here? I turn to look at the bar, praying that he's left already. Instead, I find myself looking straight into his eyes, his long fingers wrapped around a sweating glass. He doesn't look away. Just stares me down, those fathomless blue eyes locked on mine, ice cubes clinking as he swirls his drink. Goosebumps prickle under the sleeve of my cardigan, and my heart speeds up.

"Isn't it the greatest? Perfect for the discreet pick-me-up when it's been a rough day at work." When I don't respond, Lauren pokes me in the side, breaking the spell Sutton has me under. "When was the last time you had an orgasm, Soph? I know you wouldn't go on a date until the divorce was official, and the papers only came yesterday."

If it was possible for my cheeks to get any hotter, I'd give myself second-degree burns. "Two years," I mumble under my breath.

"Two years? Did you seriously just say you haven't had an orgasm in two years?"

I clap my hand over her mouth. Lauren's voice is loud enough to hear clear across the room. She wrenches free from my grasp. "Woman! How are you even alive? Also, you've only been separated for nine months. Are you telling me that Jake left you hanging high and dry for over a year while you were still together?"

"For God's sake, Lauren, keep your voice down." I will myself not to glance around. If I don't look, I won't know if Mr. Sutton is listening to this conversation. Living in denial is better than certain death by embarrassment if I turn and he's looking. Emma needs me, I can't die now.

As Lauren keeps talking, the conversation turns to all the ways my ex-husband did me wrong. Starting with the lack of orgasms, continuing to how he spent money we didn't have, and ending with the whole "sleeping with one of his model friends" that ultimately led to our divorce. I don't have the energy to interrupt so I focus on not turning around to look for Sutton.

A flash of movement in the mirror along the wall to my right catches my eye. Sutton is taking a to-go bag from one of the hostesses. I can't help watching as he pulls his wallet out of his pocket, the movement pushing his jacket aside and revealing the fact that the man doesn't skip leg day at the gym. Dragging my eyes up his body, I take the opportunity to ogle to my heart's content, the alcohol in my belly telling me it's a fantastic idea.

My gaze finishes by tracing the strong line of his jaw, a tequila-flavored voice in the back of my head wondering what it would feel like to run my tongue along it, or what that stubble would feel like against my skin.

"Shit. Sutton is staring at you, Sophie." Jess's voice cuts through my fantasy, jarring me back to reality.

I meet his eyes and all the air leaves my lungs. He holds my gaze for a moment before tipping his chin an inch, one dark eyebrow lifting with the action, grabbing his order and walking out the door.

Fuck. Me.

Two

SOPHIE

"Mom!" Emma calls from the bedroom. "Can I borrow your white wedges?"

I drag myself off the couch so I can respond without yelling. Our one-bedroom apartment is small, but that doesn't mean I want to holler across the space. "Why?" I ask, standing in the doorway.

"I was going to go to a movie with Bella and Mike." She pulls a cardigan over her crop top and jeans.

"You want to try that request again?" I give her a look. She's taken to living here better than I have, probably because she gets the bedroom and doesn't sleep on the pull-out couch like I do. The night I left Jake, she didn't ask any questions when I told her to pack her things, even though it was almost one in the morning. Just like I wasn't surprised she was still awake. No one could have slept through the shouting match between Jake and I when I discovered he'd been cheating on me.

We'd stayed with Lauren for about a month while I looked for a new place for us. Even though she'd offered to let us stay as long as we needed, once I'd been able to scrape together enough for a deposit, I'd moved us into this one-bedroom apartment. It was too small, but it was near her school so she could walk, and it bordered one of the nicest neighborhoods in Portland, so I felt safe.

Emma stops, gives herself a little shake, then plasters a smile on her face and says to me in a saccharine-sweet tone. "Mama, may I please go to the movies with Bella and Mike? And may I please borrow your white wedges?"

"Who's driving you?"

"Mike is picking Bella up now, then they're coming to get me."

"Fine, just don't stay out too late. And don't be obnoxious." It's my usual admonition to her, it has been since she was twelve and started hanging out with her friends without direct parental supervision. She's a good kid and I trust her, but teenage girls are obnoxious no matter how good they are. "What time do you think the movie will be over? It's already seven o'clock."

"I think it starts at eight so..." Her pretty face scrunches as she does the mental math. "Midnight? Is that ok?"

"Yeah, just be home right after, ok? Text me when the movie gets out, please."

Emma leans down to kiss me on the cheek. "I will." She disappears from view to pull my shoes from the back of the closet we share.

I make myself comfortable on the couch again, covering my legs with a blanket. I've got my Kindle in one hand, a glass of wine in the other, ready for a perfect Friday night. I left Lauren at work two hours ago, stuck in a meeting. "Hey Max," I say to Lauren's raggedy old cat. "She's still at work buddy." I scratch under his mottled chin. Max peers at me with his good eye, turning his cheek into my fingers so I can scratch a spot behind his ear.

Lauren and I found Max our senior year of college, a poor little kitten who'd obviously lost a fight with something bigger and meaner than him. We'd taken him to the emergency vet and gotten him stitched up before sneaking him into our campus apartment. We managed to keep Max a secret, but when Jake and I got married, Lauren kept him. He's old now but going strong. Emma and I consider him our cat too, he just never lived with us because of

Jake's allergies. Now, he happily comes to stay with me and Emma whenever Lauren is working late or goes out of town.

Max curls up on my feet, his body stretched between my calves like a sausage, a comforting warmth as I scroll absently through my phone. A knock on the door has me looking up in time to see Emma emerge, makeup carefully applied.

"Bye Mom." She kisses the top of my head as she walks past me.

"Hi Ms. Sophie." Bella waves from the door as Emma opens it.

"Hi sweetie." I wave back. "Have fun, be good."

"We will!" the girls call back as they close the door, giggling. I take a sip of my wine and settle into my book. I'm supposed to be beta-reading for one of the writers in my group, but my mind is too distracted to concentrate. Instead, I pull up an old favorite, hoping Pippa Grant's *Beauty and the Beefcake* will help me forget about the mess I've made of my life.

I'm wallowing in my feels, reading Are's voicemail to Felicity, when Lauren lets herself in the front door. "Honey, I'm home!" She pulls her shoes off. Max hops off my lap and goes to rub himself against her legs. "Hi Maxy-poo," Lauren baby-talks him, picking him up to rub her cheek against his.

"Did you guys eat already?" She makes her way to the kitchen.

"I made beef stroganoff. There's a plate for you in the fridge. And an open bottle over here if you want some." I shake the bottle of wine on the coffee table.

"I'm dying for both." Lauren brings a second wine glass. I put my Kindle down and fill it while she heats up her dinner. "What would I do without you?" Lauren sits next to me a minute later, plate in hand, already stuffing a forkful of food in her mouth. "I haven't had so many home cooked meals since college. Is it horrible of me to say I'm glad you got divorced so you could feed me more often?"

"You just missed me cooking for you." I laugh. "You did just fine without me for fifteen years."

"Don't remind me—it was a dark time in my life," Lauren says dramatically, still shoveling food in her mouth. "Whatcha reading? Anything new I should be on the lookout for?" Lauren and I were assigned as roommates our freshman year at the University of Oregon and bonded immediately when we discovered each other's secret love of romance novels. I'd dropped a pile of books as I was moving in and she'd picked up my copy of Nora Robert's *Born in Shame,* thinking it was hers.

"Nope, just rereading Ares and Felicity. I don't have brain space for anything new right now."

"Oh man, I love that one. To haikus!" Lauren and I click our wine glasses together before taking a sip.

"What kept you at work so late?" She ends up working overtime most nights, but tonight is unusually late for a Friday. I've been working there for three years as an administrative assistant after one too many clients yelled at me at the non-profit health services organization I'd been working at since we graduated. I don't mind not having a fancy title in exchange for the steady nine-to-five schedule and never having to worry about if my paycheck is going to come on time. It also means I have more time to work on my writing.

"Surprise visit by one Theodore Sutton."

I groan with her at the mention of our CEO's name.

"Is it just me or is he more bastardy than ever?" She takes another bite.

"He has been particularly grumpy this week. I'm pretty sure I heard someone crying through his ear buds yesterday morning when he walked in. What did he want with you?" I add another few inches of wine to her glass.

"It's not important." Lauren waves it off. "I don't want to think about him. How are you? It's been a week since your birthday, have you played with any of your...gifts...yet? Wait, where's the munchkin?" She looks around.

"Went to a movie with Bella and Mike. And no, I haven't. I don't exactly have any privacy around here." I shrug. "Jake texted at least a dozen times today. Called too. We did sign the divorce papers, right? I swear, I feel like I'm losing my mind."

Lauren sets her wine glass down and picks up her plate, seconds before Max hops up on the coffee table to steal a bite. "None for you

Max, this is *my* dinner." She shovels a forkful in her mouth before answering me. "You're not losing your mind. You signed the papers, he signed the papers, and I was there holding a Taser to his balls so he couldn't screw you over."

"I don't know what I'd do without you." I laugh. She hadn't actually been holding a Taser to Jake's balls that day, I'd insisted she keep it in her purse. I'd had to fight back laughter at the look on his face when she pulled it halfway out before he put pen to paper.

"You'd be fine, because you're a badass. But you know I've got your back. Want me to call him and find out what he wants?"

I snort. "Nah, it's ok. I'll call him back tomorrow. He probably needs to swap weekends with me so he can get that hair transplant surgery he always wanted."

Lauren laughs at that and refills my wine glass. We click glasses again and drain them in a few long gulps, ready for a lazy Friday night together.

The end credits of our second movie of the night are rolling when Lauren speaks up. "So....remember how I said Sutton's visit was no big deal?" Her voice is muffled by the mountain of ice cream she just shoveled in her mouth. We've been binging Hallmark movies and eating ice cream while waiting for Emma to get home. One good thing about sleeping on the sofa-bed is that Lauren and I can both fit on it. I can't count the number of times she's slept over after a Friday night of movies and wine since I moved out.

"Yeah?"

"I may have lied a little. He wanted to know who wrote the article on using our file sharing tech to create a national database of health records."

I gulp. That was one of my articles. "It's generating a lot of buzz on both sides." I'd seen some of the arguments, both for and against my point. Some were arguing that creating a national database meant more accurate health care for everyone. Doctors could access to your complete medical history no matter where, instead of the piecemeal records they had to put together from scratch every time someone went to a new doctor. Others argued it was an invasion of privacy, that the government or health insurance companies could use it to deny coverage for pre-existing conditions or track citizens who didn't want to be tracked.

Since Mailbox, Inc. is only interested in storing its users' information securely, I can see how our CEO might object to being pulled into the middle of a debate about medical privacy. I'd tried to keep my article as unbiased as possible, simply highlighting the benefits of a secure place to store sensitive records, but I guess I stirred the pot a little too thoroughly.

Lauren had been the one to approve the article and put it up on the Mailbox website. Anxiety curdles in my gut. "Shit, are you in trouble? Am I in trouble?"

"I talked him down. I'm pretty sure Sutton likes the publicity even if he'll never admit it. We've had a 50% increase in new users signing up since the article went up on Monday."

My relief is short lived when the next words tumble out of Lauren's mouth.

"He wants the author to accompany him to some gala fundraiser next week."

"Lauren!" Panic alarms go off in my head. "I can't go to a fundraiser with Theodore Sutton, he'll—"

"Know it's you?" She interrupts me. "But will he really? Has he ever even acknowledged your presence?"

"Really?" Does she not know the same man I do? "Mr. Sutton remembers everything. He's a certified genius. Of course he'll recognize me. He walks past me every morning, for crying out loud!"

"I had to give him something, Soph—he was threatening to interview the entire writing staff to find out who wrote it. I couldn't do that to them. You know what he's like, by the time he was done, they all would have quit on me."

She isn't wrong. Theodore Sutton rules Mailbox by instilling every one of his employees with a healthy dose of fear at every opportunity. Hardly anyone is brave enough to have a conversation with him, let alone flirt with him, despite how handsome he is. Some of the girls talk about it, but as far as I know no one has ever dared to do it.

"But why does he want me to go to some gala? It's just a silly blog post!" I spoon way too much cookie dough ice cream and shove it in my mouth. A second later, my head explodes in an ice cream headache. I flap my hands and squirm, jostling Lauren while I fight the pain paired with my panic over having to go to this gala with Sutton.

"There's some health insurance company big-wig who's supposed to be there. Sutton wants to see if there's any potential to your idea. He figured it would be easier to get around the corporate red tape if the conversation comes from a writer rather than the CEO."

"But I am not fancy-gala material, Lauren. What would I wear? Why can't you go?" My voice is getting higher and higher as my initial panic roars to life. I can't go on a date with Theodore Sutton, even if it is for work. Is it a date?

"Soph, take a breath babe." Lauren laughs at me. "First of all, you are abso-fucking-lutely fancy gala material. You're gorgeous. Secondly, there is no reason you can't go on a date if you want to. Papers are signed, remember?" She holds a hand up at me when I try to protest. "Thirdly, we will find something for you to wear. I'm going to be your fairy godmother." Lauren stops to think. "No, scratch that. If Sutton wants to take you so badly he can pay for a dress. Fourth, I can't go because Sutton specifically asked for the writer and he knows it's not me. I don't know the ins and outs of the healthcare system like you do. I can't fake my way through that conversation."

I want to argue but she has a point. Thanks to my years at the non-profit, I am intimately familiar with problems in our healthcare system. I try a different tactic. "I can coach you. Please, I can't go out with Sutton. I'll embarrass myself."

Lauren just shakes her head at me. "This doesn't have anything to do with Jake, does it?"

"I can't go on a date, Lauren."

"It's not a date. It's a work event. We don't even have to tell him your real name. If you're right, and he never notices you at the office, he'll never know that Elinor Price and Sophie Alexander are the same person."

Three

THEO

A COLD NOSE BETWEEN my thighs distracts me from the lines of code scrolling across my screen. Max, my rescued pit bull, pokes his nose against my thigh again, trying to get my attention. "Hey buddy, time to go out?" Pushing back from my desk, I close my laptop as I stand. Max's nails tap out a happy rhythm on the hardwood floor as he dashes to wait for me by the door. I grab his ball and leash so we can enjoy the late afternoon sunshine.

After a stop at the coffee shop on the corner for an iced latte, Max and I head to the dog park a few blocks from home. I turn on an audiobook as I toss the ball over and over for him, tuning out the crowd of people taking advantage of the sunny afternoon. This is my favorite time of day—just me and Max. No decisions to make, no one asking my opinion on anything.

Max comes bounding up to me, slobbery ball in his jaws, his lips stretched back in a doggy grin, when someone collides into my back, knocking the almost empty coffee cup from my hand.

"Oh, I'm so sorry!" a teenage girl is saying as I turn around. "Are you okay? Shit, I spilled your drink. I'm sorry, I wasn't looking where I was going." She keeps wringing her hands and apologizing profusely.

She stops to take a breath and I seize the opportunity. "It's fine, really. I was finished anyways. Are you ok?" I look her over. She's almost as tall as I am. At just over six feet, I only have a few inches on her. I can't tell how old she is, teenage girls are not something I have a lot of experience with, but I'd wager she's in high school.

"Yeah, I'm fine. Just looking for Max." She looks around, eyes never staying in one place.

"Max? Why are you looking for my dog?" I ask, confused.

"Huh? No, I'm not looking for your dog."

"You just said you were looking for Max. Is your dog's name Max too?" I point to my dopey guy who's busy rolling in the grass, his tongue hanging out the side of his mouth. "That's my Max."

"Oh. No, I'm looking for my cat." The girl's eyes dart around the enclosed space. "Have you seen a cat? He's kinda mangy looking, only has one eye and one ear?"

Sounds like a real looker. "Um, no. I haven't seen a cat. You know this is a dog park, right?"

She rolls her eyes. "Yes, I realize it's a dog park. We were making a TikTok and some dog barked at Max and he took off."

"Do you need help looking?" I offer, even though I'm sure it's not a good idea for me to be seen hanging out with a teenager in a very public place. Mailbox is already under scrutiny for that stupid blog post—I don't need to add a scandal.

"I'm okay. My friends are looking too. Are you sure you don't want me to replace your drink? I think I have some quarters left..."

I shake my head.

"If you happen to see him, just give me a shout." And with that she takes off at a jog, eyes peering around the park. My Max comes galloping up to me, drool flying.

"Where's your ball, buddy?" I reach down to scratch his ears. "Let's go look for it, huh?"

I walk back in the last direction I tossed it, eyes peeled for the bright yellow, slobbery sphere. This corner of the dog park is home to a stand of big leaf maples, branches heavy with greenery this time of year. Max and I wander into the shade of the trees, enjoying the respite from the heat. I squat down, my back against one of the thick trunks, taking a moment to enjoy the fresh air and quiet under the canopy of leaves. I don't often find this kind of peace outside my own home.

Growing up in the shadow of my famous sister, child-star-turned-Hollywood-Darling, our home was always filled with some kind of drama. Especially when our success-obsessed mother, and Casey's agent, manufactured a huge scandal that dominated the headlines of every gossip magazine for years. All I wanted to do was escape the world of Hollywood. I did so by graduating high school early and becoming an emancipated minor at the same time Casey cut ties with our mother. I ran away to college while Casey did her own thing in Los Angeles. Casey's been my only family ever since.

I stumbled into success just before my college graduation, the file-sharing program I wrote for my senior project thrusting me into a leadership role I wasn't prepared for. At twenty, I could barely remember to pay my phone bill on time, let alone be responsible for managing a team of programmers and millions of dollars of venture capital investment. But that was exactly what happened. I'd graduated from MIT and two days later sat down with Morgan Edwards, one of Silicon Valley's slickest venture capitalists, and walked out with a handshake and the promise of ten million dollars to start up Mailbox, Inc.

I'd made mistakes early on—hiring friends instead of qualified candidates, not meeting deadlines, falling for girls that only wanted me for my wallet, forgetting to show up to important meetings—until Morgan took me firmly in hand. Morgan Edwards doesn't give money away. If he invests in you, he expects to be repaid with a perfect product. In this case, Mailbox wasn't the only product—I was too. I learned the hard way to leave my happy-go-lucky nature at home when I went to the office. Ten years of practice at being "the grumpy boss" and everyone at the office is terrified of me—exactly how I need it.

A rustling overhead distracts me from the solitude. Max gives a curious, "woof," and rolls to his feet, nose pointed up. A cat is perched on the branch above my head. He's peering at me through one eye, his lone ear laid back flat against his skull. He's an ugly mottled gray and brown color with white feet. It must be the blonde teenager's Max.

"Max?" I whisper to the cat. He hisses at me and tries to back up on the tree branch. "Come here buddy, I won't hurt you." I stretch my arms towards him, my Max bumping up against my knees. Thankfully the branch isn't that high and I can reach him. I manage to get one hand on his back before he scrambles away, catching a claw in the fleshy web between my thumb and pointer finger.

"Ow!" I pull my hand back to see a deep cut through the delicate skin, blood already pooling. Damn, that hurt. "Stupid cat." The blood threatens to drip down my hand, but I have a napkin tucked in my pocket from the coffee shop. I pull it out and wrap it around the scratch, squeezing tight while I eye the cat still stuck in the tree. "Maxy boy, I think we should leave Killer up there and see if we can find that girl instead."

I step out from under the tree, trusting my Max to follow me, and scan the park. I spot her blonde hair shining in the sun, in furious conversation with another girl and a boy. I open my mouth to call her when I realize I don't know her name. Shouting "hey girl," across the park is not a good look. Instead, I jog over to the trio, hoping that the cat doesn't figure out how to get down from the tree on his own.

"Hey, I think I found your cat." I point to the stand of trees I was just under. My Max is dancing around the base of the tree, not barking, just interested.

"You saw him?" She turns hopeful eyes on me, shushing the other two teens.

I raise my hand up for her to see. "I tried to get him down but he didn't seem to like me very much."

She takes off towards the trees, her friends trailing in her wake. I follow at a distance, mostly to make sure my Max doesn't interfere.

"Max!" I call, patting my leg. "Let's go!" He walks over to me, stopping to look back at the commotion a few times. I reach down to rub his head. "Good boy." I can't decide if I should leave or stay. Standing here watching them makes me feel like a creepy old man, but I don't want to just walk away. Somehow, I feel responsible for the plight of Max the cat and his owner. I hover, undecided, until Max jumps up, planting his paws on my chest.

"Get down!" I push him off. I never did find his tennis ball, dammit. I look around, hoping to catch sight of it. I circle the grassy stretch between me and the trio of teens still trying to coax Max the Killer Cat down from his perch. Stepping into the shade of the trees, I spot our tennis ball behind the thick trunk of the maple where I was sitting.

"Emma! There you are!"

I freeze. I know that voice. What the hell is Sophie Alexander doing here?

"What's going on?"

"Sorry, Mom. I'm just trying to get Max. He's too scared to climb down."

"He's not scared, he's mad. Go away, give him space."

Now I'm stuck, I've been here too long, standing like a dummy. If I move now I'm going to look like a creeper who was hiding back here spying on her and her kid. I glance around, looking for my Max. He's off on the other end of the fenced park, running like the big dope he is. I stay still, hoping she doesn't notice me, thankful that the tree trunk is wide enough to keep me from her view, I hope.

If I thought being seen with a random teenager would be bad for my reputation, being seen with an employee and her teenager would be even worse.

"Hey big man, it's okay," Sophie croons. I panic for a split second, thinking she's talking to me, until I realize she's talking to the cat. I relax against the trunk. Her voice is a little rough around the edges, like she just woke up.

My dick twitches at the thought of that voice, that rough, hushed, voice in my bed one morning. Of course, I grin to myself, I probably wouldn't enjoy the words that are actually coming out of that mouth, but the thought of that sleep-roughened whisper in my ear has blood pooling in my southern hemisphere.

"Come on Max, you have to come where I can actually reach you," she's saying. I don't dare peek around the trunk of the tree. Sophie's image flashes in my mind and I push it away. Just because she smiles at me every morning when I walk in the door doesn't mean she wants anything to do with me. Even if I caught her checking me out at the restaurant last week. And I definitely shouldn't have anything to do with her. Especially since I can't get the conversation I overheard between her and Ms. Masterson at the restaurant out of my mind.

Two years? No wonder she got divorced. And good riddance.

"Gotcha! Ow!" The triumph in her voice melts into annoyed muttering. I grin to myself, imagining her scolding the ugly cat, as the voice fades away.

I emerge from behind the tree just in time to see Emma following a tiny blonde through the gates of the dog park. Sophie's hips sway temptingly with each step, a long, floral dress sweeping the ground as she leads the way. I stare for a long minute before reining myself in. I need to get out of here.

Four

SOPHIE

"SHIT." I SUCK IN a breath as hot coffee spills onto my thumb, burning me. "He didn't see me did he?" Just my luck that when I sneak upstairs to get coffee from the fourth floor, Mr. Sutton is the one waiting for the elevator when the doors open in the lobby.

"Of course he saw you, you were standing right in front of him."

"That's not what I meant. Did he see me trip?"

"I don't think so." Thank God. The last thing I need is him remembering my face before I'm supposed to go to this gala with him. I straighten out my blue and yellow dress and check to see if coffee got on my cardigan sleeve before I take my seat at reception.

"Good morning Tina." I smile at the girl sharing the desk with me this week. I've been here for three years while the seat next to me has been a rotating string of doe-eyed college graduates. They never stay for long, sometimes being plucked upstairs to be assistants to the various higher-ups, sometimes leaving for greener pastures. I've had a few offers to go upstairs, but the idea of changing jobs is overwhelming. Since my split with Jake, most days it feels like I hardly have enough time to do the bare minimum to keep Emma and I above water. I don't think I could handle yet another major change.

Also, I like being in the middle of the action and the people-watching is great. Between our own revolving doors and the streets of Portland outside, it's a writer's smorgasbord of interesting characters.

I nod at the pile of packages covering the desk between our seats. "Tina, can you take those to the mailroom?"

Tina fills her arms with the packages and scurries away. I give it a week before she notices the cart the mailroom leaves for us to bring them packages.

Lauren sets her giant purse on the desk next to me. "You know I'm going to have to give him your answer today. You'll do it, right?"

"I don't know..."

"Please Soph? Just think, you'll have delicious food, schmooze a bit for Sutton, then free drinks all night long. Don't you think you've earned a night on the town after everything you've been through? It's time to celebrate your freedom." She doesn't say it, but there is an implied fact that going out to a fancy gala like this is something that Jake could, and would, never have done with me. "Come on, Soph, when are you ever going to have a chance like this again? It'll be fun. Well, mostly fun."

"What about Emma?"

"What about her? She can have a girl's night with Aunt Lauren, or a sleepover with a friend."

I suppose I'm being ridiculous. "Fine. I'll go."

"Yes! Thank you Soph, you're saving my bacon here!" Lauren does a little twirl and kisses me on the cheek, about to dash to the elevator.

"Wait!" I grab her by the arm and pull her close. "I have conditions."

"Whatever you want." Lauren's grin is inches from mine.

"He's not picking me up. I'll meet him here."

"Done. I wouldn't want him knowing where I live either."

"He never knows my real name."

"Obviously."

"No social media."

"Tricky, but I can at least promise that there won't be any inter-company coverage. Mr. Sutton hates to be photographed anyways. I can't promise though, there'll probably be press at the event, I can't control that."

"Last thing—*I* get to pick out my dress. I don't trust you not to dress me in something completely slutty and inappropriate."

Lauren pouts. "Can I at least help you pick? Otherwise you'll ruin all my fun."

I smile at her. "Fine, you can come with. But I have final say."

"Deal!" Lauren drums her hands on the edge of my desk. "We can make it a girls shopping trip and bring Emma too. You know she'll love that. Leave it up to me!" With that, she grabs her purse and heads to the elevator bank. "Morning Julian." She smiles at the security guard and chats with him while she waits for the next elevator to arrive. Slipping inside as the doors open, she blows me a kiss before the doors close on her.

"No, Mom, not that one."

"Why not?" I turn to look at myself in the mirror again. I love the soft mint color, the billowy long sleeves, and the loose pleated skirt that swishes against my legs. Besides, I could pair this one with flats and a cardigan and it would be perfectly appropriate for work. Bonus points for a dress I can get good use out of.

"I'm with Munchkin on this one. This is a $2,000 a plate gala, you can't wear a dress you would wear to the office. Next!" Lauren pushes me back into the dressing room. "Strip. This time, *I'm* picking."

I reach around to unzip the perfectly nice dress. "I don't see why I can't pick something that is at least a little bit practical." I grumble to myself as I struggle to undo the zipper. I can't quite reach my arm far enough to get a good grip on the zipper pull, I keep reaching and the pesky little sucker pulls out of my grasp every time, leaving me turning in circles trying to get it.

"Emma!"

Her blonde head pops through the curtain, a cheeky grin on her face. "Yes, Mother? Did you need assistance?"

"You were peeking weren't you?"

"Can you blame me? You look like a chihuahua chasing its tail." Emma can't hide her giggles, despite my best mom look.

"Just unzip me, please."

My not-so-Mini Me grins over my head in the mirror while I scold her. "A chihuahua? Really? I know I'm fun-sized, but there's no need to rub it in."

Ever since Emma shot past me in eighth grade, she's lorded the extra five inches she has over me. At five foot two, I'm resigned to a life of step stools and using tongs to reach things on the top shelf. Just as she finishes unzipping me, Lauren comes back holding a bright blue sheath dress in her hands. I eye it warily.

"That's never going to fit me. I have these things called hips and boobs." I emphasize my point by grabbing the offending body parts. The only article of clothing Lauren and I can share are shoes—she's tall and willowy, while I'm what polite society would call curvy. My hips and thighs mean business.

"Yes it will, trust me." She shoves the dress at me. "Just try it on, please. And hurry up, I have to pee."

I stick my tongue out at her before I flick the dressing room curtain closed and step into the dress. I send up a silent prayer of thanks that when we stopped at the house to pick up Emma I didn't take the time to change out of my work clothes and still have my shapewear on. The slinky blue fabric slips over my thighs and hips with surprising ease. Maybe Lauren wasn't crazy to grab this one. I pull it up over my stomach, sliding the delicate cap sleeves over my shoulders.

I stall, enjoying the feel of the silky fabric and the perfect fit, not daring to look at myself in the mirror, half-listening to Emma and Lauren flipping through TikTok on Lauren's phone.

"Mom! Hurry up, I'm starving."

"Fine, here!" I fling the curtain open, hand on my hip. Emma and Lauren's open mouths and stunned expressions are the only response I get. "What?"

"Sophie. That's it. You have to pick this one." Lauren is the first to recover.

Emma finds her voice and claps her hands like the little girl I remember. "Mom, you look so good!"

I step out of the dressing room so I can look in the big mirror at the end of the hallway. I stand as tall as I can and eye myself. I haven't worn a dress this tight since before Emma was born, but it doesn't look as bad as I expected. The fabric hugs my body, a low dip in the front of the dress somehow doesn't make it feel like my boobs are going to fall out at the slightest breeze. I twist to look at the back and grin at the way the dress shows off my assets. "You think so?"

"Seriously, Mom? You look hot!"

"Well, you don't have to sound so surprised." I tweak Emma's nose when she huffs at me. The action catches the price tag under my arm. Curious, I pull it out to look. The bile that rushes up my throat is instantaneous. I freeze, afraid to breathe too hard. "Oh my God. Oh my God. Lauren. Take it off. Take it off me right now." My words get faster and louder with each syllable.

"What? What's wrong?" Lauren is at my side in a blink, hands waving over my body, searching for the source of my panic.

"Look. At. The. Tag," I grind out between my teeth. I'm holding as still as possible, terrified if I breathe too ambitiously I'll damage the dress.

"Sophie, you scared the shit out of me. That's not funny. You gave me a heart attack, woman!" Lauren doesn't seem at all concerned about the number of zeros printed on the tag.

"Lauren, there is no way I can afford this dress. It's three *thousand* dollars!" I hiss. "I didn't even pay this much for my wedding dress. Help me get out of it, please." I can't help the tears that well up in my eyes. I love this dress. I love the way I look in it, but this is exactly why I was afraid to let Lauren pick—she never looks at price tags until after she's fallen in love with a dress. We've been scraping by for so long that the idea of spending more than a hundred dollars on a dress makes me want to throw up.

"Calm down Soph." Lauren laughs at my panic. "I told Mr. Sutton if he wanted your company at the gala he was going to have to pony up for the dress." She reaches into her purse and pulls a matte black credit card out of the pocket. "You realize that he probably pays more for a bottle of wine."

"But..."

"Nope. You're getting this dress." Lauren's voice drops. "Sophie, you look amazing in it." I can't help glancing in the mirror again at Lauren's words. "When was the last time you did *anything* for yourself? Theodore Sutton isn't going to care. This is pocket change to him. You, my friend, deserve to have a night out, looking and feeling as gorgeous on the outside as you are on the inside." Lauren wraps her arms around me and squeezes tight for a moment. The tears that had welled up at my panic slip down my cheeks.

It's been so long since I was the one being taken care of. Between Emma's health issues as a toddler and tip-toeing around Jake, taking care of myself has been my lowest priority for so long I don't think I know how anymore. But still, I can't accept this dress. It's too much.

"I get final say. And as much as I love this dress, I'm not getting it. I can't Lauren. I just can't. Go find me something else. Preferably something that costs less than my rent." I gently push her towards the racks of dresses to look for something else.

Emma pops up from her stool the second Lauren walks away. "Why won't you get this one Mom? You look amazing. Don't you think you deserve to feel like a million bucks for one night?" She shakes her head in disbelief that I would choose not to let someone else buy me this dress.

"No sweetie. I wouldn't enjoy myself, no matter how good I looked. The whole time I would feel like I owed Mr. Sutton something because he bought me such an expensive dress." Emma opens her mouth but I shush her. "No. It's not right and you know it. I can't accept something so expensive, especially if he doesn't even know what he's buying. It doesn't matter if he would think it was expensive or not. *I* think it's too expensive, so I could never enjoy it. End of discussion. Why don't you go help Lauren look?"

I step back into the dressing room and take one last look at myself before sliding the dress off my shoulders and hanging it back up. I meant what I told Emma and Lauren. I would never be able to enjoy the evening knowing I owed so much to a man who didn't even know my real name. And it feels wrong to let a man who isn't my husband—ex-husband—buy me something so expensive.

I pull my phone out while I wait for the girls to come back with more dresses. There's a few emails from Emma's school, a reminder for Emma's annual checkup, and a text from Jake.

> ***Jake****: Hey, I really need to talk to you. Can you please call me?*

I stare at the message, turning my options over in my mind. I could ignore him. But then he'll just keep sending them and sending them. If he's really in a mood, he'll start sending them to Emma too. Ugh. I just want him to give me space, I don't want to deal with him right now. The papers are signed, what more does he need? Why can't he just leave me alone?

"Mom?"

A beautiful deep burgundy dress comes sailing over the top of the dressing room. It's very similar in style to the blue one, but with velvet accents at the bust instead of a ruffle. Before I pull it on, I check the price tag. It's a much more reasonable three figure number. It's still more than I would ever spend on myself, but at least I won't feel like a high-paid escort in this one.

Five

THEO

"Mr. Sutton?" Mercedes, my assistant, pokes her head into my office. I peer out from behind my monitor, tapping one earbud to pause my podcast so I can hear. "Lauren Masterson is here to return your card."

"Send her in." I straighten my tie out of habit and pull both earbuds out. Assessing the state of my desk, I opt to stay seated rather than get up. Sometimes perching on the edge of my desk affords me an extra aura of power, but I won't need it for this meeting. She could have just left my card with Mercedes, but I need her intel on this Elinor woman.

Lauren steps into my office, glancing around. "I, uh, brought your card back." She swallows audibly. "And the receipt."

I hold my hand out to take them from her. "I trust that an acceptable outfit was found?" How much of my money did she spend?

"Yes, sir." A little more confidence slips into her voice at this. "S—Elinor was very grateful for your assistance with the purchase."

"Please let her know that the limo will pick her up at eight o'clock sharp. Do you have an address for me?"

Ms. Masterson bites her bottom lip before answering, eyes darting to the art on my walls. "She'd rather not share her home address. Would you object to picking her up from here?" Seriously? What does this woman think I'm going to do?

Heaving a sigh, I nod. "Fine. I'll pick her up here, even if it is exceedingly out of the way." I smirk to myself, letting Lauren interpret that how she pleases, knowing I made my word-of-the-day calendar proud.

I turn back to my computer, but the woman doesn't leave. "Was there something else you needed?" These lines of code aren't going to write themselves. I have a dozen very well-paid people downstairs who could write this code for me, but this is a personal project, one I don't want anyone else to touch yet.

"Er. It's just..." At my raised eyebrow, Lauren swallows and gets on with it. "Elinor isn't used to going to events like these. She's nervous. Could you...maybe you could try and be nice to her?"

"Are you insinuating I'm not nice?" I raise an eyebrow at Ms. Masterson, daring her to contradict me.

Although I never intended to be completely unapproachable, years of having to prove myself as a businessman, and overcome my early notoriety, have taken their toll on my personality.

Granted, it's lonely up here on my own, but if everyone is scared of me I won't be tempted to make the same mistakes I made when Mailbox was starting out. And I definitely don't want this writer getting the wrong idea about me. I didn't ask for her to come with me because I needed a date. I don't date.

I learned long ago that women don't see *me*, they see my wallet.

"My apologies, sir. I didn't mean to imply you weren't capable of being nice. But Elinor is nervous, and as her manager it's my job to look out for her." Lauren pulls herself up to her full height and glares at me. Ms. Masterson has spunk.

Hiding my smirk, I pick up the receipt on the desk. "I promise to be *nice*. Thank you." I don't wait to watch Ms. Masterson walk away. Instead, I scan the paper in my hand for the total.

Three hundred and fifty dollars? That's it?

I asked Elinor Price to come with me because Morgan Edwards is going to be there. If he sees me without a woman on my arm I'll hear about it at our next meeting. According to Morgan, "men of means only go to these events alone to signal one thing—their bed is empty for the next contender." And of course, Morgan will happen to have a niece or a cousin or a colleague's daughter who would be just *perfect* for me. They always turn out to be silicone-enhanced, money-craving leeches who can't hold a conversation to save their life.

I was supposed to take my sister, but her husband whisked her away on a surprise vacation, sans kids, to Bora Bora. His next movie starts production soon and he'll be stuck filming in the middle of the desert for months.

Besides, the charity is for the children's hospital and Elinor's article about potential uses for Mailbox in the medical community happened to stir up a lot of buzz I want to take advantage of.

The afternoon drags on as I work on my project. I let Mercedes screen the emails coming to me, knowing she'll tell me if there's something I need to stop and handle. The best thing I ever did was hire her. Morgan complains that I pay her too well, but she earns every penny of that six-figure salary as my literal and figurative gatekeeper.

"Mr. Sutton?"

"Yes?"

"It's five o'clock. I'm heading home, and you need to get ready for the gala."

Looking out the floor-to-ceiling windows to my left, the sunny summer sky gives me no clue what time it is. I was stunned my first summer up here in Portland when the sun didn't start to sink until well past nine.

"Right, thank you Mercedes. Have a good evening."

Mercedes is the only person in this building who isn't scared of me, not that she has any reason to be. She's the best assistant I've ever had, anticipating my needs and taking care of the minutiae I don't care for. Plus she keeps me from working late too many nights a week and doesn't take any shit from me, no matter how grumpy I am. I'm not looking forward to her retirement in a few years.

After tidying up my desk, I head downstairs, making sure to punch in the code that keeps the car from stopping on any other floors. It's the one hard and fast rule of this building—I do not share the elevator. Ever.

"Good evening, Mr. Sutton." Julian, the daytime security officer, says as I pass him. I nod in acknowledgement, my eyes glued to the back of the blonde who just walked out the door. My eyes lock on to the sway of her hips as I put my hand on the door to exit the building.

"Julian." I remember before I walk through the glass door. "I'm picking up an Elinor Price here this evening. Let Rex know would you? She's to be allowed to wait inside if she arrives before me, and I'll need him to make sure she gets home safely afterwards."

"Yes sir. I'll make sure he knows."

Satisfied, I hurry to my car so I can take Max for a run before showering and getting ready for this gala. At least it's a Thursday night so I'll have an excuse not to stay too late. Nothing good ever happens after midnight.

Happily tired from our run, Max settles into his bed, eyeing me as I pull a tuxedo out of my closet and lay it out on my king-sized bed before stepping into the shower without waiting for it to warm up.

The sway of Sophie's hips haunted me through the entire five mile run. I've known who she was since her first day at Mailbox, the woman who smiles and greets me every morning when I walk in, the only one who never cowers or attempts to flirt.

Her first day, when I'd opened the front doors and stepped into the lobby, everything was different. Usually, when I step inside everyone in the building freezes, just like I've trained them to. Walk into a room snapping loudly enough at someone on the other end of your phone and, eventually, people cower, terrified to be on the receiving end of your wrath. Not her.

No, Sophie Alexander had looked up at me with a serene smile. Her pink dress and yellow sweater matching the happiness oozing from every pore of her sweet face. Just like today, her sunshine gold hair was braided in a crown. It should have looked ridiculous, a grown woman looking like a milk-maid, but it fit her. I'd had to work to keep my usual scowl on my face as I walked past her, a smile threatening to escape at her greeting.

That's when I noticed the glint of a wedding band on her left hand. From then on then I'd ignored her, ignored the tug in my chest at the sight of her. But since seeing her at the restaurant and then again at the dog park, Sophie keeps popping into my mind at the most inconvenient times.

Too tired to fight it, I let my mind wander where it will. Hand braced against the tiled wall, I close my eyes and let the water stream down my back. Without conscious thought, I grip my cock, stroking absently as visions of Sophie fill my mind. Her blonde hair catching the morning sun as I walk in the door, the late afternoon shadows creeping across her pink cheeks as I leave in the evening. My hand slides along my length, squeezing lightly. The way she props the door open when the weather is gorgeous, a spring breeze sending a lock of hair to caress her cheek.

With a groan, I fist myself, pulling and squeezing as I think of her. In my mind, the warm water running down my arm and under my fingers is the warmth of her mouth. Her pink lips wrapped around me, taking me in. A tingle starts in my toes, running up the back of my legs.

I throw my head back, the water streaming down my chest now, like fingers trailing over my skin. I imagine her in the shower with me, the cool tile against her back, her gasp that I'd swallow with a kiss. I'd delve into the warm recess of her mouth, her tongue captured by mine.

That damn pink vibrator I'd seen her open at the restaurant torments me. Is it waterproof? I'd run it along her collar bones, before tracing it in circles around her areolas. The vibrator on one, my lips on the other. My teeth pulling and nipping at her rosy pink nipple until it stood to attention, begging for me.

Gasping at the thought, my cock throbs with need, the end dripping with my desire for this woman. I fist it hard, tugging the way I want to tug on her breast.

Sophie.

Her name rings in my ears, swirls in the steam of the shower. Tempting me, floating through my body. She's so short, I'd pick her up, sliding into the silky cocoon of her pussy. Her back against the shower wall, her legs wrapped around my hips. Those long fingers that fly across her keyboard would dig and scratch into my back. That sugar-sweet exterior melting before her absolute need for me to fill her.

I pump my fist faster and faster, chasing the release I know is coming.

How loud would she scream my name if I pressed that vibrator to her clit while I fucked her against the wall? Would it send her beyond the ability to form words in that sweet mouth?

What's hiding behind that innocent exterior? If her husband hasn't satisfied her for two years, is she desperate for release?

Would she whisper my name as she came? Or scream it?

"Teddy."

Just imagining her whispering my name sends me over the edge. The need that's been building at the base of my spine explodes. My legs buckle under me and I see stars as I come, my arm braced against the tile the only thing holding me up.

Shit. I shouldn't be thinking this about an employee. I've been so careful over the years to never allow even a hint of scandal at Mailbox.

Showered, dressed, and fed—both me and Max—I pour myself a finger of whiskey while I wait for the limo to arrive. Max gives me some side-eye from his spot on the floor as I slide my jacket on and button it.

"What do you think, Maxy? Do I look like an orca? Or a penguin?" I hold my arms out and turn for him. He huffs and rolls over, tongue hanging. "That bad, huh?" I fish out a treat for him from the stash by the door and retreat to the couch to wait for my driver.

Forcing myself to forget about Sophie, I focus on the evening at hand. Who is this mysterious writer, Elinor Price? I've seen her articles on our company blog before, she has a concise yet lyrical way with words that I admire, even if her topics tend toward the pop culture that I avoid—there are only so many articles a man can read about his sister's love life. But then, that must be what she was assigned to write by Lauren, so who knows if that's truly where her interests lie?

I'm intrigued by her. I'd looked at the receipts Ms. Masterson left, she'd bought a three-hundred dollar dress and a fifty dollar pair of shoes. That was it. Elinor Price could have spent whatever she wanted and it was a fraction of what I expected.

I let a sip of the golden liquid slide down my throat, burning down to my stomach. I don't intend to drink much tonight, you never know what can happen when going out with an unknown variable. But I have a feeling I'm going to need something to take the edge off my sudden fascination with the receptionist and help me get through another long evening with a virtual stranger.

"Night, Max. Behave." I admonish my derpy mutt as the limo arrives. Polishing off the last of my drink, I set the glass down in the kitchen sink and stride out to the limo. Time to get this over with.

Six

SOPHIE

"Are you sure this is going to work?" I haven't worn a dress this tight or this short since we were in college and the stiletto heels Lauren insisted I buy pinch my toes with each step. I'll probably have a blister by the end of the night. The giant ring on my right hand, *not* the vibrator one, has me feeling off-balance and self-conscious, and my face is itchy from the heavy makeup Emma applied.

"Yes I'm sure. It works for Superman, it'll work for you." Lauren looks me up and down as we walk. "And why are you whispering? It's literally just us." She waves her hand around the empty parking lot.

"I'm nervous, okay? And I'm not used to these." I wave at the glasses perched on my nose. "They feel weird."

Lauren stops me as we get to the front door of Mailbox. Hands on my shoulders, she forces me to look her in the eyes. "Listen to me, Soph. You look amazing. That dress is fucking gorgeous on you. I made you shave *everywhere*, so I know you feel sexy under there."

When I open my mouth to protest she just gives me that look, the one I know so well, the one that tells me to shut up and grow a pair.

"Your makeup is amazing and that updo is fabulous. You look nothing like the cheerful ball of sunshine everyone expects when they walk into the lobby. You're a sexy goddess. The glasses just make it harder to recognize you. You can do this."

"But—

"No buts. Here." She hands me a small flask. "Have a sip while we wait."

I unscrew the top and take a cautious sip. The smooth, smoky taste of Glenfiddich coats my tongue. Relieved it's not the tequila Lauren prefers, I take another generous sip, letting the warm heat of it settle in my stomach.

"Keep it." She pushes it into my hand when I try to give it back. "I have a feeling you might need it more than me."

"Ma'am?"

Rex, the night security guard, is standing in the doorway. "Are you Elinor Price? Mr. Sutton said I was to let you wait inside. If you want," he adds, stepping back to let me through.

"See," Lauren leans close to whisper. "Rex doesn't recognize you and you see him at least a few days a week." Without waiting for me to respond, Lauren steps inside the building. "Hi Rex, we'll wait inside, thanks."

"I didn't realize that both of you were going with Mr. Sutton," Rex glances between the two of us. While I'm dressed to the nines, with my hair twisted up in a fancy updo, Lauren is rocking a pair of leather leggings and a flowy tank top. She looks ready for a night of bar-hopping and fun. I look like I'm ready for a night of small-talk and finger food.

What I really want is to be curled up on the couch with my pajamas and my laptop, writing.

"Do you want me to wait with you?" Lauren asks once we're inside.

"No, you go. I'm a big girl, I can wait all by myself." I walk toward my desk, intending to check my email while I wait, when Lauren pulls me back sharply. "Don't give yourself away dummy. Elinor doesn't work at the front desk." Her whisper is harsh and I freeze, sheepish. Technically, Elinor works completely remote and has never even visited the office in Portland.

Changing direction, I pull out my phone and sit in one of the plush chairs dotting the lobby. I don't actually think I've ever sat on one of these before. They are surprisingly uncomfortable.

"Bye! Have fun, please!" With an air kiss, Lauren is out the door and on her way for a night of fun with Emma. With nothing else to do, I scroll through my phone, ears tuned for the sound of an approaching car.

I'm about to absently tap like on a photo of a couple getting engaged, the girl looks vaguely familiar, when I freeze.

No.

What the fuck?

I stare at the photo, not believing what I'm seeing. Jake. On one knee. Holding out a ring to some twenty-something baby.

Every muscle in my body locks in place as I stare, dumbfounded, at the photo. The caption catches my eye.

"I've been waiting for this day for two years, can't wait to be your wifey and raise this baby with you."

Two years?

The court mailed me the divorce papers a week ago.

Emma and I moved out nine months ago.

Two mother-fucking, orgasmless, forced to listen to him fart in his sleep, years.

I'm not sure what's responsible for the bile rising in my throat—the fact that my ex-husband just proposed to his girlfriend of two years when we've been divorced for all of a week, or that she looks closer to Emma's age than ours and says shit like "wifey."

Wait.

Baby?

"Ma'am? Are you okay?" Rex's voice echoes in my ears as a cold sweat breaks out over my skin. My mouth waters and my stomach heaves. Clapping a hand over my mouth, I dart to the nearest trash can and promptly lose everything in my stomach. I haven't eaten so there isn't much, but the smell of my own vomit, laced with that last shot of whiskey, has my eyes watering.

Leaning against the nearest wall, I breath in through my nose, attempting to calm down. Keeping my eyes closed, I focus on letting my stomach settle before I move again.

"There's a bathroom right over there, if you need it," a gruff voice says quietly from above my head. Great. As if this night couldn't get off to an even worse start.

I open my eyes and look straight up into the blue ones of Theodore Sutton. He doesn't look angry, more like disappointed, or maybe resigned is the better word.

"Thanks." I push myself off the wall and take a wobbly step towards the bathroom. "I'll be right back." I escape to the lobby bathroom before I can make even more of a fool of myself. Bypassing the sink, I go straight to the janitor supply closet, to the secret stash of toothbrushes and travel-sized toothpaste I keep stocked back here. Mercedes, Sutton's assistant, orders it in bulk for his private bathroom and gives me some to keep in the lobby for emergencies.

As I brush the taste of vomit out of my mouth, I inspect my face for damage. Thankfully, all I need is to reapply my lipstick. The smoky eyeshadow Emma applied is still intact, my pale blue eyes popping against the deep navy she used, and my hair hasn't budged.

Brushing my teeth helps, the minty taste and smell focusing my brain on something other than the painful mental math of Jake's new relationship. I refuse to let him have any power over me. I am Sophie "gave birth without an epidural even though I wanted one" Alexander. I did that and I can do this.

Betrayal, despair, anger, and utter sadness all war inside me. I want to go home. I want to forget. I want to cry and I want to scream. Most of all, I really, really, really want a drink.

Instead, I take a deep breath, straighten my dress and push open the bathroom doors. Rounding the corner into the lobby, I pause, taking in the sight in front of me. Theodore Sutton has his back to me, his hands tucked in the pockets of his very well-fitting tuxedo pants. He's staring out the window at the brilliant sunset lighting up the sky. I can't see his face, but the golden light dances over his dark hair and shoulders.

Mr. Sutton turns to look in my direction, the sunset throwing his face into shadow. I'm too far away to get a good look, but I swear he recognizes me for a moment. But that's impossible. Lauren promised I look nothing like my usual self with my tight dress, heels and glasses. Besides, it's not like he knows who I am. Sure he knows my name, but he knows everyone's name at Mailbox. He's got that whole genius thing going on. Just because he remembers my name doesn't mean he actually notices me at work.

I'm only the receptionist.

"Are you alright?" Mr. Sutton strides towards me, his head cocked to one side. He usually walks through the lobby with his shoulders back and his head high, as if he owns the place. Because he does. He hasn't lost the aura of power and authority that he always has, but it's tempered by something else right now. He looks exhausted.

"Elinor?"

Realizing I haven't said a word yet, I swallow hard. "Yeah. Yes. I'm okay."

"Should I have the limo take you home?"

I'm mesmerized by his face as he speaks. I don't actually think I've ever heard him speak so kindly. When he walks through my lobby he's always yelling on the phone, or telling someone off.

Do I want to go home?

Yes.

But I think about what's waiting for me there. Emma, who's going to ask why I'm not out, and she won't stop until I tell her. I can't tell her this. Not until I talk to Jake. Oh God. I have to talk to Jake.

Not tonight.

I'm not going home. I'm going to go to this stupid gala, forget about what I just saw, and definitely overindulge in both food and drink before I get dropped back home and my Cinderella moment ends.

Smoothing down my sides to give my fluttery hands something to do, I clear my throat. "No, thank you. I'm ready to go, Mr. Sutton."

"Theo."

"What?"

"You don't have to call me Mr. Sutton all night long. Theo is fine for this evening." Straightening his bow tie, which I hadn't noticed until now, he offers me his arm. "If you're sure?"

Nodding, I take his arm, feeling steadier on my feet as soon as my fingers close around his warm biceps. "Goodnight, Rex." Mr. Sutton—Theo—tips his head and leads me towards the door.

The July evening is still bright and warm as we step outside, but a cool breeze off the Columbia River keeps it from being uncomfortable. The lushness of the city has always been one of my favorite things about living here. Growing up in the dry, asphalt-covered metropolis of Southern California, I always longed for the greenery described in my favorite books. Arriving in Oregon for my freshman year of college was a revelation, and I've never looked back.

Mr. Sutton opens the door to the limo, stepping back as I awkwardly slide in. I haven't ridden in a limo since my senior prom, and the floor-length gown I wore twenty years ago was easier to navigate than the much shorter dress I'm wearing tonight. "Settled?" Mr. Sutton asks—I can't call him Theo in my head, I just can't—sliding in beside me.

I nod, not sure what to say. My mind is still racing, but I need to push it all aside for the sake of tonight.

Tonight, I'm Elinor Price, writer and badass.

Elinor isn't divorced. Elinor didn't just find out her ex-husband is engaged to a woman young enough to still be on her parent's health insurance. Elinor takes no shit from anyone, not even Mr. Scary here. *Especially* not from Theodore "I'm an alpha male" Sutton.

I wonder if there's champagne or something in this limo?

"So, Lauren tells me you've been writing for us for the last few years. I had a look at some of your past articles and while the topics may not be my cup of tea, I did find your writing style quite enjoyable."

Quite enjoyable? I thought Sutton was in his early thirties, not his eighties?

"Thank you. I've enjoyed the opportunity to be part of the writing team at Mailbox." God, I sound as bad as he does. At least I have the excuse of complete and utter mortification to sound like I have a yardstick up my ass. "Lauren mentioned the gala was a fundraiser, what organization is it for?"

"It's for the children's hospital . That was part of the reason I invited you to accompany me. After all the buzz your article created about using Mailbox for storing medical records, I wanted to put some feelers out to the hospitals and local doctors to see how they felt about it.

"And the insurance companies too, right?"

"If possible, yes. Although, please be sure to speak only on your own behalf and not on behalf of the company, I don't want them thinking we're making promises we can't keep." The look he turns on me should be scary. Brows drawn, blue eyes piercing, every inch of my skin under his scrutiny. It's the same look I've seen him cast on department directors, vendors and competing software CEO's—the look that's earned him a reputation as a shark in business.

But I don't melt under his gaze. I don't tuck my tail and squirm. Maybe it's because, at this point, it feels like everything that could possibly go wrong already has, and I have no fucks left to give. Maybe it's the way his eyes drop to my lips for a split second. Instead of frightening me into submission, his steely gaze lights a fire in my belly.

Straightening up in my seat, I stare right back. "I'm not an idiot, sir. I know not to make verbal agreements on a night like tonight. I'm well aware that I am just a lowly—" I catch myself before I say receptionist, "writer. I promise not to embarrass the company, Mr. Sutton. Is there anything else? Would you like me to walk two feet behind you at all times? Or never let your glass sit empty?"

Some of Sophie's pent up anger at Jake is leaking out into my Elinor persona, but I'm too pissed off to care. Sutton leans back in his seat, regarding me with narrowed eyes. When I don't look away, a lazy smile spreads across his features, cracking the grim set of his mouth.

"My God," he murmurs, almost too quiet for me to hear over the noise of the limo. "You are something else Ms. Price. And no, that won't be necessary, you may walk where you like—behind, beside, in front, or even away from me. And I'll be sure to get my own drinks." Sutton finishes with a smirk as he settles into the plush seat.

Chastised, I sit back as well, fiddling with my phone clutched in my hands. I turn it over and over, afraid to unlock it and see what else the universe is going to throw at me tonight.

A large, warm hand closes over my own, stilling me. "Did something on your phone upset you earlier?" His voice is surprisingly gentle. A tightening in my throat warns me not to relax.

"Could you," I begin, but stop and clear my throat before I finish the thought. "Is there somewhere I can leave my phone? I... I don't think I want to have it on me tonight."

Sutton regards me for a moment, then takes the phone from me. "I can hold onto it for you, if you like." At my nod, he slides it deep into the inside pocket of his tuxedo jacket. "Just let me know when you want it back."

We spend the rest of the drive in silence, staring out the windows. I have no idea what's going through his mind, but mine is a mess. Flashes of memories torment me. Every time Jake was working late or at a photoshoot. Me laughing with Lauren that he would never cheat on me because he has no game. My utterly misplaced confidence that my husband was as faithful to me as I was to him. I've been down this road before—I knew he cheated on me—it's why Emma and I moved out in the first place.

But I'd convinced myself it had been a one-time thing. A fleeting moment. The reality that my dope of an ex-husband, with his beer belly and greasy face, had been in a relationship with this stunning twenty-something for *years* is a blow to my ego. While I was home, curled up with my book boyfriends, feeling guilty about it too, he was out with a real live girlfriend without sparing a second thought for my feelings.

I'm a fool. Doubly a fool for believing that our vows meant something. I close my eyes and wish Jake was here so I could yell and scream at him.

"We're here," Sutton's deep voice pulls me back from the spiral of emotions warring inside me. "Shall we?"

Seven

THEO

SOPHIE, OR SHOULD I say Elinor, pauses for a moment before taking my hand and stepping out of the limo. Why Sophie is masquerading as Elinor Price is beyond me. I don't know if Lauren set this up as some kind of joke, but after watching Sophie puke in the lobby I keep waffling between being disgusted that she's already had so much to drink, and worried about her.

I hide a grimace when she slips a flask out of her little purse and takes a swig. This is going to be a long fucking night.

"Let's do this." Sophie/Elinor stands ramrod straight, her purse clutched in her hands. I offer my arm again, not sure if she'll take it, but she slides her fingers around it without hesitation.

Thinking of the flask I watched her slip back into her clutch, I lean down to whisper in her ear. "Have you eaten tonight?" If she's going to insist on drinking, I'm going to insist she eat. Having watched her empty her stomach out into the trash can, pouring alcohol into her is only going to make this night messier. I should have insisted the limo take her home.

"I'm fine." From her expression, you'd think there was a statistics exam waiting for us inside, not an evening of small talk and finger food. Squaring her shoulders, Sophie lets go of my arm and enters the hotel ballroom, leaving me to follow.

I didn't get a good look at it until she stepped out of the limo, but the dark red dress she's wearing looks like it was poured on her, highlighting her hourglass shape. While her hips and breasts are generous, her small waist begs for me to wrap my hands around it. The clothes she wears at work don't hide her shape, but they don't highlight it the way this dress does. Her usual June Cleaver look has been replaced by a bombshell, the glasses only adding to the mystery. Does she actually need them? Or is she trying for a reverse Clark Kent/Superman disguise?

I shake my head and we make our way around the room, navigating the banal chit chat of a few hundred moneyed souls, on an indirect path to the bar.

There's a band playing softly in the corner. No one is drunk enough to start dancing yet, but it will happen sooner or later. Usually, I try to leave before some blonde in a tight dress and ridiculous heels traps me into dancing with her. But tonight...no. I stop that thought in its tracks. Letting myself fantasize about her in the shower was a mistake—the line between employee and boss is becoming too blurred in my mind.

"Are you normally this quiet?" Sophie interrupts my musings.

"As a general rule, I speak when I have something to say."

"Not when you have questions? Surely even the mighty Theodore Sutton deigns to learn about the people around him? Or are we plebeians not worthy of your attention?" The second the words leave her lips her eyes go wide. I hold still, determined not to react. Her hands clap over her mouth, stifling her gasp. "I can't believe I said that!" Her words are muffled by her hands, but I hear them loud and clear.

She's just one more woman who sees me as nothing but a suit with a wallet. A robot without feelings. Instead of retreating, like instinct tells me to do—hide, protect, don't let her near your inner self—I wrap my icy facade closer around me and look down my nose at her. I should never have let my guard down in the first place. Watching her from afar was obviously not enough to discover her true colors. "Are you finished, ma'am?"

Tears fill her eyes, the golden green depths of them swimming. "I'm so sorry, sir. I don't know what came over me. I didn't mean that, I just..." She swallows hard, finally lowering her hands from her mouth. Her hands grip my forearm, stopping me from walking away. "I was angry at someone else and I took it out on you. I'm sorry. Truly."

The remorse in her eyes is clear, but the damage is done. Women want me for one thing and one thing only. Not that I expected this to be anything other than a business dinner, but for a moment, a flicker of hope had passed through me.

For a moment, I thought she was different, that this was a woman who might actually see me for me. But she'll never see me as anything other than Theodore, self-made-billionaire or Theo, younger brother of Casey Sutton, America's Sweetheart. I shove my disappointment down into the depths of my soul, where all my other heartaches live, and tip my head at her. "Consider it forgotten." My voice is wooden, but at least it's polite. "Shall we?" Again, I offer her my elbow, leading her towards the bar. I'm going to need another whiskey if I'm going to make it through the evening.

"Whiskey, neat," I say as soon as I catch the bartender's eye.

"Make that two please," Sophie says when I indicate she should order. Something kicks in my chest at her words. I don't know what I was expecting her to order, maybe a vodka soda or something lighter, but I'd be lying if the thought of her swallowing the whiskey, the burn of it sliding down her throat, doesn't turn me on. I push the thought away. I'm Theodore fucking Sutton, time to act like it.

When she's not shooting her cutting words into my soul with sniper-like precision, Sophie is every bit as charming as I expected her to be the moment I realized who she really was. She chats with everyone who crosses our path. From insurance executives and other high-profile donors, to their arm-candy dates, she talks to everyone with the exact same kindness and genuine interest. She even strikes up a conversation with one of the waitresses handing out glasses of champagne. I've never been to one of these things with a woman who wasn't sizing up every other female in the room as competition, or mentally comparing the size of my wallet to every other available bachelor in the room. Irritatingly, she doesn't seem to be interested in me at all.

But sometimes, when we have a moment alone, she gets this faraway look in her eyes and a blanket of sadness settles briefly around her shoulders.

It's driving me crazy.

It must have something to do with whatever upset her earlier, and yet, she's completely tight-lipped about herself. As the evening drags on I realize she only ever asks about the people around us, never offering up any tidbit about herself. The more she doesn't say, the more I want to know. This tiny blonde, with curves that beg for me to touch them, doesn't say a word about herself all evening.

I've seen her nearly every day for years and all I know about her is her name and her penchant for wearing bright colors. She's a mystery I want to solve.

A mystery with an ass I want to bite and full red lips. Her breasts are cupped lovingly by her dress, but all I want is for my hands to be the ones lifting and holding them. I don't know what this woman does to me, but I can't stop fantasizing about her and it's annoying as fuck. I don't have time for this.

"Theo?" Morgan is saying as I drag my thoughts away from Sophie's ass.

"What?" I'd been watching the way her hips swing gently from side to side as she walked away from our table and hadn't heard a word Morgan had said.

"I said, that is a fine-looking woman you brought with you tonight. Where did you find her?"

Counting backwards from fifty in my head to try and force some of my blood flow back towards my brain, the real one, not the little one, I take a sip of water to buy myself time. "She's one of the writers at Mailbox. She wrote the article about using Mailbox for storing patients' medical records, the one getting all the buzz right now.

That's why I brought her tonight. I wanted to see what the reaction was here at the hospital before taking any steps to either embrace the idea or guard against it." I shrugged. "That she's attractive wasn't the point."

I pull my carefully practiced persona back into place. The aloof billionaire, the genius, the man so smart he doesn't have the patience for a conversation with just anybody. Morgan is one of the few who knew the real me back before Mailbox became what it is. He helped me trade in Teddy Sutton, lonely programming genius, for Theodore Sutton, business mogul and eligible bachelor. There are days I hate him for it, but being the cold-hearted bastard I'm known as these days has saved me more money and heartache than my very well-paid CPA.

"A writer, huh? Be careful—they get wordy on social media when you break their hearts." He tips his glass of scotch in a salute. My whiskey turns sour in my gut, curdled by his words. "So what is the buzz? Are you going to pursue it?"

"Elinor got into an interesting discussion with Brett Carney about the hospital's current records storage."

"Carney?"

"He's the head of IT here at the hospital." I wouldn't have known that if Sophie hadn't struck up a conversation with the man. He looked woefully out of place, his obviously rented tux ill-fitting and worn at the shoulder seams, the button straining to hold the jacket closed over his belly. It was his wife that Sophie spoke to first, complimenting her shoes and wiping the anxious look off the woman's face.

"What the devil is the head of IT doing here?"

"Apparently, their oldest daughter was treated here for leukemia over thirty years ago." I shake my head at Morgan's curious look. "She passed away, but according to Brett's wife, he kept fixing the computers at the nursing station while they were here and got himself a job while they were treating her."

Before I can tell him any more of the interesting story, Morgan cuts me off with a question. "So what was so interesting about him?"

Does he even know how callous he sounds? Probably not.

"The hospital has an internal medical record storage software—Carney picked it out himself—but they haven't been happy with it. The files are unwieldy, and they can't embed photos, videos, or anything else to the record. It has to be uploaded separately and then a note made. He was complaining about the doctors always forgetting to make a note and then calling his department in a panic because they can't find the file after the fact."

This gets me an appraising look in return. "And you think you can solve that problem?"

Taking a sip of the whiskey I've been nursing all night, I nod. "I know I can. And make it more user friendly for the doctors. Whoever designed that software designed it for other IT people, not the actual users."

"You've got that look in your eye, son. Is this going to make me money?"

I shrug. "Who knows? I have to design it first."

"You have to design what?" Sophie slides into the chair next to me, a fresh glass in her hand. How many drinks has she had? I can count at least three, this makes four, since we've arrived. That doesn't include what she was taking sips of in the limo.

Morgan answers for me as I study the glass in her hand. "Theo here is always getting ideas. It's whether or not he can make money off them that matters."

Is it a vodka soda? Or maybe a gin and tonic? It's clear, but has some kind of carbonation. She already puked once tonight and I have no desire to deal with it again. I'm well aware that I'm vacillating between thinking the worst of Sophie and admiring her conversational skills. Are she and Ms. Masterson trying to pull one over on me? Is this some kind of ploy? Deep down, I have to wonder if she's drinking so heavily because she doesn't want to be here. Especially with me.

She wouldn't be the first woman to drink her way through a date with me.

With that thought, I've had all I can take of this evening. A glance at my watch reveals it's not too early to make an exit, thank fuck. Turning to Sophie, I lean close, my lips nearly touching the shell of her ear. I can't help myself, even if she'd rather drink her way through the evening than converse with me.

"I'm ready to leave. Did you want to finish your drink before we go?" At my words she pulls away, eyes wide, then she wraps her lips around the straw in her glass and sucks it down. Her cheeks hollow out and all I can picture is her doing the exact same thing but on her knees, with my cock between those luscious lips instead of a cheap plastic straw.

Something of my thought must show on my face because she ducks her head and mutters as she sets the glass down on the table. "It's just seltzer. They didn't have any tap water at the bar."

Well, I wasn't expecting that one.

"I'm ready to leave when you are."

I can't keep up with this woman or my own thoughts. Is she humoring me? Playing hard to get? She's either entirely oblivious to the effect she has on me, and every other man in this room, or she's a master of the game.

Standing, I take my leave of Morgan before offering her my elbow. Weaving our way through the crush, I can't help noticing that the farther we get from the gala, the slower Sophie walks. Is she reluctant to leave? Or exhausted from the evening? I've flip-flopped between concern, irritation, awe, and judgment of this woman so many times in the last few hours that I can't tell what my opinion of her is anymore.

"Thank you." Her quiet words startle me from my thoughts as we wait at the valet stand for the limo to arrive. Her back is to me, the smooth slope of her neck dancing in front of my eyes. A short tendril of escaped hair catches my eye, daring me to sweep it aside.

"I'm sorry I was such a mess when the evening started. It's been...a rough day. I hope I didn't disappoint you. I tried my best." She finishes with a shrug that turns into a shiver in the cooler evening air.

On instinct, I slide my jacket off, draping it around her shoulders. I follow that by running my hands down her arms, my need to touch her stronger than my sense of self-preservation.

"You were just fine." The reassuring words slip off my tongue as easily as my hands slide back up her arms. That rogue tendril of hair caught in the collar of my jacket begs to be tugged free, and I give in. Gently, I pull it loose, the tips of my fingers grazing the back of her neck. Her soft gasp at my touch is my undoing, the vulnerability in it calling on every instinct I have to help her. I don't even know what from, but I don't care.

I'm saved by the arrival of the limo. Wordlessly, I open the door for her and she climbs into the backseat, sliding over to make room for me. "Do you want to talk about it?" I surprise myself that I genuinely want to know, before we've pulled away from the curb.

"Talk about what?" The darkness of the interior feels like a confessional of sorts, the streetlights flickering across her face. A place where secrets can be safely shared.

"Whatever upset you this evening. Before the gala." I add.

"I really shouldn't tell you, it's personal."

"And I'm your boss."

Sophie nods at my words, bottom lip caught between her teeth, indecision written all over her features.

"Your scary boss," I add, hoping to elicit a smile from her. Which I do. It's a tiny smile, but a smile nonetheless.

"What I really want is to forget about it. Just for one night. I don't want to be... me. Is one night too much to ask?"

Eight

SOPHIE

I DON'T KNOW WHY I asked it, other than this whole evening has been a roller coaster of emotions and all I want is to make it stop. I don't care how, I just don't want to be Sophie Alexander tonight. Making small talk, chatting as we walked through the crowd, I could pretend to be Elinor. But the moment it was just me and Mr. Sutton, it all came rushing back. Sitting here in the dark, in this limo, it threatens to overwhelm me again.

My ex-husband cheating on me for far longer than I knew.

The picture of him down on one knee, promising her the sun and the moon when he couldn't even tell me he'd be home for dinner.

And I can't deny the pull I feel towards Theo. If you'd asked me this morning, I would have said he was nothing but a cold, unfeeling shell of a man, who delighted in the way his employees scatter from his presence like cockroaches from a light. I've never heard him speak a kind word to anyone in the lobby, but then, I've only ever heard him on the phone, berating whoever dared to disappoint him that morning.

The Theodore Sutton I knew from work wouldn't have asked a mere IT guy and his wife thoughtful questions about their sick daughter, nor would he have been so kind and sympathetic to her passing, even if it was over thirty years ago. The Theodore Sutton I imagined wouldn't have made sure to put our empty whiskey glasses with the other dirty glasses on the bar top, he would have just left them wherever he felt and let someone else clean it up.

The Theodore Sutton I pictured would not have given me his coat jacket or steered me so carefully through the crowded room. And the Theo Sutton who passes my desk every morning never has this desperate, vulnerable look in his eyes, like I'm holding the keys to a treasure he's hunted for his whole life.

"Elinor..." The way he growls the name lights me up like a firework. Tonight, I'm not pathetic Sophie Alexander, mother, forgotten ex-wife, doormat. I'm Elinor fucking Price.

His eyes keep searching my face, looking for something. I don't know what, but the moment they drop to my lips, the fire inside me roars to life. One moment, I'm sitting in my seat, the next I'm straddling Theo's lap, my fists buried in his crisp white shirt, his lips fighting with mine. His tongue and mine battle for dominance, his teeth nipping at my bottom lip until, with a growl, he cups my ass and pulls me closer. Theo reaches between us and gently removes my fake glasses, setting them on the seat beside him without ever breaking the connection between us.

I gasp as his thickness presses against my heated core, a sensation I haven't felt in years. He takes advantage of my gasp to delve in, devouring my lips like a man starved.

Like an itch I could ignore until that first delicious scratch, the pressure of his hard cock against me is irresistible. I grind my hips, chasing the sensation, desperate for more.

"Yes. Use me." Theo growls against my lips as I chase the orgasm twisting up inside of me. My fingers pull at his bowtie and the button beneath it. It's been so long, so fucking long. I'm desperate, the breathy moans escaping me the only sound I make.

Theo's hands squeeze my ass, pulling me against him. Between the rocking of the limo and the rocking of my hips, it doesn't take much more to push me right to the edge. Theo's hands slide down my thighs, his fingertips slipping under the edge of my dress. "I want to touch you. I want to feel you come on my fingers. I don't care about anything else. I just need you right now." Theo's words penetrate the haze of lust in my mind, his hands sliding inside the edge of my dress, freezing me mid-moan.

Reality crashes in around me, the tight fabric of my dress stopping my thighs from spreading farther apart and the layers of my Spanx a barrier to the friction I truly want. I throw myself off his lap, desperate and on the verge of orgasm, the flush of arousal turning to the burning of embarrassment the second the cooler air of the A/C hits my cheeks.

"No, no, no, no, no," I mutter to myself, burying my face in my hands, embarrassed tears leaking between my fingers. I did not just grind on my *boss* in the backseat of a limo. With Spanx on.

"What's wrong? Elinor?"

I don't know which is worse—the concern in his quiet words or the hand that's gently rubbing my back. Rubbing it the same way I rub Emma's when she's upset. Because I'm a mom.

I'm a woman who has to wear control-top shapewear under the dress her date, her *boss*, paid for. Who borrowed makeup from her best friend just to look somewhat acceptable at an event someone like Mr. Sutton attends so often he owns the very expensive bespoke tux he's wearing. The tux that had my mouth watering every time I glanced at it all night. This isn't a Cinderella evening—this is a joke.

Taking a deep breath to stop my tears, I straighten up. Too mortified to face him, I angle my body to look out the window instead as I try to fix my twisted dress. "I'm sorry. It's not you." I can't help looking back over my shoulder at my lame excuse. Sutton can't school his features quickly enough to hide the momentary hurt that flashes across his face before it transforms into the hard expression I see every morning. "I need to go home."

Thankfully, we're almost back to the Mailbox headquarters. The few minutes it takes us to arrive are thick with unsaid words. I can't speak, the lump in my throat my excuse. Mr. Sutton silently hands me back the glasses, but I don't put them on, just slip them inside the clutch I rescued from the floor of the limo. Just as silently, I hand him back his jacket, even though all I want is to bury my nose in it and breathe in the vanilla and whiskey of his cologne. I forgot how good a man could smell—Jake always smelled slightly sweaty.

Sutton doesn't say a word until we pull into the parking lot. He has the door open and is halfway out before turning back to announce, "I have work to do. The limo will take you home."

"My car is right—"

He cuts me off with a dark look. "You've been drinking. You're not driving home. The limo will take you." Without waiting for me to respond, he steps out and closes the door in my face, walking inside without a backward glance.

My mind whirling, I fish the flask Lauren gave me out of my clutch and take a long sip. God I'm a mess. He's right, I shouldn't be driving right now—I'm not drunk, only pleasantly buzzed—but if I was in my right mind I would never consider it. This is all Jake's fault.

"Ma'am? Where am I taking you?" The driver's voice echoes through the silent interior. I rattle off my address and lean back in the seat. Not caring about the hangover I know I'm going to regret in the morning, I spend the ride home polishing off the flask of whiskey. I'm determined not to think about what just happened, even though I can still smell our arousal in the air and my thighs are rubbing together, desperate to finish what we started. The more I drink, the more needy I become. By the time the driver pulls up at my front door, I'm almost crying from my need to find release.

I scramble to let myself in, grateful that Emma is spending the night at Bella's house. I couldn't face her right now. I flip on the shower then strip out of my dress, peeling everything off me with a sigh of relief as I wait for the water to warm up. The humid air in the bathroom settles on my skin as I pull bobby pin after bobby pin out of my hair. When did that piece at the back escape? I bet it offended the mighty Mr. Sutton all night, one more bit of evidence that I'm not cut out for evenings like tonight. I'm just a middle-aged mom who needs to remember to stay in her lane.

But I can still feel the ghost of Theo's hands on my body, the way his fingers trailed down my back, lighting up my skin with each touch. I step into the shower remembering the way his hands buried themselves in my hair, angling my face just right as he kissed me, tipping my head back as he trailed his lips along my jaw. The heat from the shower burns where his scruff was rough against my skin and I savor the pain, treasuring the evidence that for a moment in time someone wanted me.

I try to ignore the ache between my legs as I go through my usual shower routine. Eyes closed, I definitely am not imagining Theo's strong fingers rubbing the shampoo into my scalp in place of my own. The water droplets running down my neck aren't his lips trailing kisses behind my ear and across my collarbone. The loofah brushing across my nipples *isn't* his soft touch, and when my hand cups my breast, rolling the hard peak between my thumb and forefinger, there's no way I'm picturing his hand instead. Especially when I find myself reaching down between my legs, the throbbing need only made worse by the warm water. The quiet moans I can't contain are barely audible over the water pounding against my body.

Abandoning the loofah, my fingers go to work, circling and rubbing my clit. I haven't done this in so long, I can't even find a rhythm that gets me anywhere as close as I was in the limo. Tears of frustration threaten as I slow down, letting the hot water of the shower pool in my palm before trying again. The heat of the water helps but isn't enough.

I consider climbing out and getting the vibrator that Lauren gave me, but the thought of having to clean up whatever wet trail I create after I'm done is enough to stop me. Slapping the shower wall in frustration, I open my eyes to find the loofah and finish showering.

I can ignore the ache. I've been doing it for years—what's one more night?

"Would it be completely unprofessional to leave my sunglasses on all day?" Even my voice sounds hungover as Lauren and I walk through the door at Mailbox.

"Yes. But you can drink as much coffee as you want and we'll go get something greasy for lunch, okay?" Lauren waves as she heads to the elevator. Since my car was left here last night, we carpooled to work and I'm running late, courtesy of a frantic search for my phone this morning. Lauren and I tore the place apart looking for it to no avail. I have a horrible suspicion it's still in the coat pocket of one Theodore Sutton. If I could afford to abandon it there I would. But right now, I'm too queasy to figure out how to retrieve it.

Dropping my purse on my desk, I rush around the lobby, checking the lights are on, magazines set out correctly, and that Julian has everything he needs for the day.

"Morning, Sophie." He salutes me with his usual coffee, steam drifting up from the plain black mug. "Fresh pot upstairs." Julian presses the elevator call button for me. Each floor has its own break area except mine. There is a coffee bar in the corner but it's for clients only, not staff. Besides, the best coffee is on the fourth floor—their office manager was the manager of a local coffee shop for years before she was hired here.

"Thank God, I need it desperately. Is Tina here yet?"

"I haven't seen her." Julian nods. "I'll keep an eye out while you run upstairs."

"Thanks!" I step into the elevator.

Ten minutes later, I have a steaming cup of gloriousness in my hands as I wait for the elevator to take me down to my desk. With a ding, the doors open. The too hot, but so delicious, sip I was in the middle of taking tries to kill me as I sip and inhale in shock simultaneously. *He's* standing there, my phone in his hand, glaring at the doors as they open.

Shit, shit, shit.

I can't die now, death by coffee is an undignified way to go.

"Did you need something?" Mr. Sutton, Theo, the man who had his hands all over my body last night, says without a hint of recognition.

I shake my head, turn on my heel and head for the stairs. Four flights of stairs is nothing compared to being stuck in a confined space with him. I don't think he recognized me, but I can't afford to let him get a closer look. My hair is down, the fake glasses are tucked safely in a drawer at Lauren's house and I'm back in my normal floral dress and cardigan combination. I don't want to be late to get to my desk, but I can't face him, not after last night.

As I make my way down the stairs as fast as I dare, I can't help wonder why Sutton was headed *down* the elevator when this is the time he normally arrives. Did he leave something in his car? I didn't notice if his Audi was parked in its usual spot near the door when I arrived, I was busy impersonating a vampire by keeping my eyes on my feet as I followed Lauren in.

My question is answered the moment I push through the stairwell door and see the elevator doors closing on his face. I'm directly opposite him as they close, allowing me to catch his unguarded expression for a moment. My heart whacks against my ribs at the hurt in his eyes, my stomach turns over and I can't breathe. Hurt? Why would he be hurt? He's the one who slammed the limo door in my face last night.

"Sophie!" Tina's unexpected call startles me into sloshing coffee onto the cuff of my cardigan. Damn it.

"Good morning, Tina." I fake my usual cheerful greeting, hoping she's not going to be too chatty this morning. At least not until I get a chance to drink what's left in my mug and eat one of the granola bars I have stashed in my snack drawer.

"Guess what?" Tina's voice has the conspiratorial note of someone who's got juicy gossip to share. "You'll never guess what Mr. Sutton just dropped off."

"How about you tell me, since I'll never guess."

"He dropped off a phone!" Tina bounces with glee to have the inside scoop. "It was his date's last night and she left it behind in his jacket pocket. He dropped it off on your desk and said Lauren from Content would know how to get it back to her." Tina starts walking away to share her news with Julian. "Oh!" she turns back to me. "And he said not to power it on. She turned it off for a reason and he intended for her to get it back that way. Isn't that just the sweetest?"

He brought my phone back. I almost wished he hadn't, that I could just walk away from the earth-shattering information that's waiting for me when I turn it back on. That I could just leave it and pretend it never happened.

Instead, I put the phone, my phone, in my desk drawer, determined to ignore it for as long as possible. My morning passes quickly, fielding phone calls, spam calls and real calls alike, directing visitors and helping Tina get packages mailed out. I'm in the middle of helping one of the admins from accounting print labels when Lauren appears at my desk.

"Ready to get lunch?"

"Yeah, just give me one minute to finish this." I keep clicking on my screen, emailing the finished labels back.

Tina pipes up before I can grab my purse. "Did you hear?"

"Hear what?" Lauren perches on the edge of my desk, always ready to hear the latest gossip in the office.

"Sutton went on a date last night and she left her phone in his jacket pocket! He brought it down this morning and said to give it to you since you helped set them up."

I cough, shocked at how the story has been twisted.

"So? Who is she? How on earth did you manage to set Mr. Sutton up on a date? And can you set me up with him too?"

"Come again?" Lauren's raised eyebrow is lost beneath her bangs. "I definitely did *not* set Sutton up on a date. I would never do that to my fellow womankind."

"Bye, Tina," I interrupt. "I'll be back in an hour."

"Don't forget the phone!" Tina reaches over to my desk but I intercept her and pull the phone out, handing it to Lauren before she can say anything else.

"Thanks!"

I follow Lauren out the front door and down the block to our favorite Mexican place, Uno, Dos, Tres, before she speaks. "So...you wanna tell me why it turns out The Bastard-in-Chief had your phone?"

"Um, not really?"

I follow her inside the restaurant, the colored lights and bright decor creating a cozy atmosphere, the smell of fajitas banishing the queasy churning of my stomach. Suddenly, I'm starving. I follow Lauren to one of the high tables at the bar, knowing we'll get in and out quicker, not because we're intending to do a Mad Men and have one of their lethal margaritas with our lunch.

Although, I'm tempted.

"Soph, come on. Talk to me."

"Food first, talking after."

Thankfully, the waitress stops by with chips and salsa at that moment, saving me from having to elaborate. We both order the two tacos lunch special and a water, even though now that I have to tell Lauren what happened, that margarita sounds even more tempting.

"Jake just got engaged."

"What?" Lauren chokes on the chip she just ate, thumping her chest and coughing while her eyes water. I don't say anything, just nudge her glass of water closer and wait for her to recover.

"That tiny-dicked fucker is engaged? To who?"

I swallow, not wanting to say it out loud. "Some girl. I don't even know her name, but she posted a photo of him proposing and said they'd been together for two years. Two. Fucking. Years." I take a long sip of my water to stop the tears that threaten me. I refuse to cry over Jake.

"Wait..." The mental gears are turning in Lauren's mind, I can see it on her face.

"Exactly. I thought it was a one-time thing when I saw that receipt for the flowers, remember?"

Lauren nods. "Of course I remember. I still can't believe that fucker was dumb enough to use your account to order them for someone else. Did he really not realize that you'd get the confirmation email, with his note attached?"

As dumb as it sounds, he really was that stupid. When the confirmation email first showed up in my inbox I'd purposefully ignored it, not wanting to ruin my own surprise. But when the delivery confirmation email arrived and I had no flowers, I'd gone to check and make sure he'd gotten my work address correct.

Imagine my surprise when the flowers I assumed were in celebration of our anniversary had this note attached.

Last night was amazing, can't wait to do it all over again next weekend. Love, Jake

The next weekend. The weekend he'd told me he was going away for a golf trip with the boys. The golf trip that I'd written extra articles to pay for.

Yeah. There's a reason that was the last straw in our marriage.

"It gets worse."

"How can it get...no. Tell me it's not what I think it is." Lauren's normally tan skin goes pale.

I hesitate, then rip it off like a Band-aid.

"If you're thinking that the new fiancée is pregnant, then you would be correct."

She stares at me in stunned silence. Saying it out loud is worse than just thinking it. Makes it real. Makes it something I can't just pretend never happened. Especially now that I've told Lauren. "Oh my God. Soph. I don't..." She swallows hard. "I don't know what to say."

The way her voice cracks on the last word is what breaks me. Tears fill my eyes and spill over before I can stop them. Dabbing at my cheeks with a napkin, I'm too worried about stifling my sobs to notice Lauren's gotten up until her arms are wrapped around my shoulder, hugging me tight.

"I'm going to kill him. I'm going to pluck his balls off and feed them to him. No, I'm going to cover his ball hair in honey, then set a swarm of bees on him. Wait, no I have a better idea, I'm gonna hire a hitman to pull a Game of Thrones on him, except he'll start by plucking his ball hairs out one by one. *Then* he can cut off his junk and feed it to him in a hot dog." Lauren's muttered plans for revenge wash across my head as she holds me. The last one gets a wet and disgusting laugh out of me.

"I got the text right before Sutton picked me up. I turned my phone off and gave it to him to hold onto for me. I haven't looked at it since. I don't know if I can."

"Do you want me to look for you?" Lauren offers. "Hang on." She pulls her phone out and taps a few buttons before holding it up to her ear. "Tina? Hi, it's Lauren from Content. Hey, Sophie isn't feeling well, I'm going to take her home. You're okay to cover the rest of the day, right?" She pauses for a moment, listening to whatever Tina is saying. "Thanks Doll, I'll let her know. I'm sure she'll be fine in the morning. "

Putting her phone back in her purse, Lauren catches the waitress's eye. "We're gonna need a couple of margaritas."

Nine

THEO

I NEED A FUCKING drink.

And a shower. I haven't left the office since the limo dropped me off last night. After Sophie practically threw herself across the limo to get away from my touch, I walked into my office and started working on the medical file sharing program that sparked in my imagination last night.

Thanks to the private bathroom attached to my office, I was able to freshen up this morning. When Mercedes found me passed out on my office couch this morning, she tossed a spare change of clothes on me and pointed to it. At least she took pity and got me a coffee from the fourth floor, handing it to me before going over the day's agenda.

Yawning, I look at my calendar, not seeing anything vital for the afternoon. "Mercedes," I call through my open door. Knowing it will take a moment for her to walk over, I start tidying up the papers strewn across my desk.

"Yes, Mr. Sutton?" Mercedes is at the door, waiting for me.

"I'll work from home for the rest of the day." What I really mean is, I need a nap, some food, and my dog. Poor Max. I know that my house cleaner will have let him out this morning when she arrived, but I feel terrible for abandoning him.

"I don't see it being a problem."

"Can you call in an order to that Mexican place down the street for me? I'll pick it up on my way home. Just leave the tux, I'll have it sent to the cleaners later." I start to collect up the notes I'll need to work from home when I realize another problem. I don't have my car, the limo picked me up from my house last night.

"I don't mind..."

"No Mercedes, we've discussed this before—my laundry is not your responsibility. I'll walk down to the restaurant."

"Very good, see you tomorrow sir."

The walk to Uno, Dos, Tres clears my head of the fog from last night's fitful sleep. Why am I so worked up over this? Do I have any right to be angry that Sophie showed up instead of Elinor? That Sophie *is* Elinor? The moment I saw her there instead of a stranger, I'd let my guard slip, and she'd promptly cut me down to size. She only agreed to go to the gala because I made her. I have no right to be upset that she pulled away, even though it lit a fire in me I can't shake.

Pushing open the door, the delicious smells have my mouth watering. The familiar strains of instrumental music are barely audible over the hum of chatter. "Picking up for Sutton," I tell the hostess before she can open her mouth to speak.

"It'll be just a few minutes, sir. Do you want to wait in the bar?"

Since I have to wait for my Uber to get here, having a quick drink while I wait strikes me as an excellent idea. I make my way to the bar, perching on a stool without bothering to glance around. The main restaurant is busy with the lunchtime rush, but the bar is fairly empty. A few groups are perched at the high tables dotting the area, but no one else is brave enough to belly up to the polished wood bar. Probably afraid of someone telling their boss.

"What can I get you, sir?" The bartender slides a small napkin toward me. "I'm just making a batch of our famous margaritas, if you're interested?"

"Who on earth is having one of your lethal margaritas at this time of day?" I can't keep the judgment out of my voice. It's one thing to have a glass of wine or a gin and tonic over a lunch meeting, but one of these margaritas? You might as well order an appointment at the unemployment office with a side of Alka-Seltzer.

"Someone who's having a really bad day." He jerks his chin towards a table I hadn't noticed, tucked behind a pillar. One of the women has her back to me, her blonde hair obscuring her face. She's slumped over against her friend, obviously upset. The friend is leaning down, whispering something to her with a fierce look on her face. I'd hate to be whoever she has her sights set on. My balls shrink in sympathy for whichever man is responsible for the tears at their table. It has to be a man—nothing else could reduce one woman to tears and the other to her defense like that.

Straightening, the friend turns to look at the bartender. I know that face. Ms. Masterson levels me with a glare before recognition dawns on her face and she ducks behind the pillar. I want to laugh at the fear I saw in her eyes.

The blonde.

If that's Lauren, then the blonde must be Sophie. Is it *my* balls being threatened over there? I can only hope it's Sophie's ex-husband's instead.

"Gin and tonic please. And put their order on my tab." The words are out of my mouth and my card is sliding across the smooth, sanded bar before I can second-guess myself. "You don't need to tell them it was me."

I don't know what has Sophie so upset, but the idea of her having a bad day doesn't sit right in my gut, not after last night. With her reaction to me sitting heavy in my mind, I'm tempted to take my drink and join them, but it's obvious they don't need a stranger, and a man at that, crashing their party.

Instead, I content myself with sipping my drink and scrolling through my email while I wait for my food. I'm not *trying* to overhear their conversation, but now I know it's Sophie, I can't help listening to her distinct voice.

"All those times I sent him on his way with a smile..."

"I just can't believe he would..."

"Do you know a good lawyer?"

"I think Nancy in accounting does."

Why does she need a lawyer? Aren't they already divorced?

I manage to contain my curiosity for another thirty seconds, until a quiet sob penetrates the noise of the restaurant. I'm on my feet before I realize what I'm doing, a few long strides all it takes to arrive at their table.

"Ladies," I clear my throat. "Is there anything I can do to assist you?"

Lauren stares at me like a kid caught with their hand in the cookie jar, silent. I shift my gaze from her face to her companion, the cardigan-clad, floral-wearing ray of sunshine, currently trying to bite her lip hard enough to stop it from trembling. I don't know why I'm here, or why I care. I should leave. Just grunt, scowl for good measure, and walk the fuck away.

Rage at whoever hurt this woman builds inside me and I battle an irrational need to sweep her up in my arms and carry her away from here.

"No, but thank you Mr. Sutton," Sophie mumbles, wiping her eyes with a napkin before tossing it on the pile building up on her side of the table.

"Sir?" someone says from near my elbow. The hostess hands me my order, neatly packaged up, before I register what's happening. "Do you ladies need anything?" she says to the other two, walking away when Lauren shakes her head.

"Did you need something?" Lauren is asking me as I stare at the bag of food in my hand. "We were kind of in the middle of a private conversation." She indicates the pile of wet napkins on the table. "I already called the office and Tina is fine on her own for the rest of the day. I can finish up my day working remotely."

For the sake of my reputation, I brace myself for the words I'm about to say. I hate them before I've uttered them, but if I don't say it I'm going to take this tearful woman home with me and try to solve all her problems with the one thing I have—my wallet. "Nice to know you've covered your asses for this afternoon's little day-drinking field trip. Do you also have excuses ready for tomorrow's hangover? And what about a ride home?" I can't help the last question. I'm being an asshole, but I need to know they're going to get home safe.

Sunshine sniffs loudly, straightening in her chair. "Listen, Mr. High and Mighty. Per company policy, we are allowed to use our PTO for whatever reason we need, as long as we clear it with HR. Which Lauren did. I am taking a personal day and that's all you need to know. Now, if you'll excuse me, I have a margarita to drink and twenty-four hours to forget. But first, I'm going to the ladies room."

With that declaration, she slides off the high stool and walks away without a backwards glance. That sway, those hips. I'm halfway across the restaurant before I realize I've followed her. Hanging a left at the hostess stand, I step out into the bright sunshine to wait for my Uber.

Fuck.

Ten

SOPHIE

FULL GLASS OF WINE, expensive(ish) dark chocolate, a sexy playlist ready to go on my laptop and...crickets. The cursor blinks, mocking me, but no words appear on the screen.

I even scrolled through all my favorite male models Instagram and TikTok accounts for "inspiration" and I've got nothing. Lauren complained that I left her hanging at the end of chapter six. Well, my characters left me high and dry at the end of chapter six as well.

I'm so tired of myself, of my own life. All I want to do is escape into the world I created and forget about my own shitty one for tonight. I don't want to think about Jake and his new fiancée, or how I'm going to tell Emma. How do you tell a fifteen-year-old that her dad is starting a brand-new life without her in it? I'm still ignoring my phone, terrified of what I'm going to find if I look. That's a problem for Tomorrow Sophie. Current Sophie's only concern is finishing this chapter.

"Do you want to come up?"

Jessie, my imaginary photographer, and Cody, the damaged rockstar who just took her on a date, are just standing there. Staring at each other. Does Jessie go inside? Do they have the wild monkey sex I love to read about, but haven't been able to write a word of? I don't know, and no matter how hard I try, I can't picture what happens next.

Some aspiring romance novelist I am. I can't even get them to kiss for fuck's sake.

Frustrated, I nibble on a piece of chocolate. Lauren dropped me off hours ago, full of food and margaritas, and empty of tears, before scooping Emma up and taking her out. Sadly, Lauren has always been more of a parent to Emma than Jake, especially in the last few years. I waved them off before falling into a tequila-induced nap. I woke up an hour ago, fuzzy-mouthed and ready to distract myself.

With Emma gone and the apartment to myself, when am I going to have a better chance to work on this sex scene? Even if I feel anything but sexy at the moment.

I push back from the coffee table. Maybe a change of scenery will spark something. I head to the bathroom and turn on the faucet. A long, hot bath should knock something loose. While the tub fills, I sort through the mess on the floor, tossing Emma's clothes on her bed and putting mine away. I don't know what's harder, my own lack of personal space or Emma's natural teenage messiness.

The hot pink gift bag, containing both the best and most embarrassing gifts I've ever received, taunts me from the closet where I left it last week. I pull the books out and slip them onto my bookshelf. Lucy and Annette's books go alongside the rest of my collection, the craft book on the lower shelf. Next to another copy of the same book.

Knowing what elements should be in my book isn't the problem. My problem is that it's been so long since I've felt anything close to sexy that I can't even imagine it for my poor couple.

For a split-second last night I'd felt that spark. The dress helped, so did the way Sutton's eyes roamed over my body, those dark eyes burning my skin in those few moments he let his guard down. I know I didn't imagine the way his hand hovered above my ass all night, as if he was barely restraining himself from touching it.

Two years. I wasn't exaggerating. Jake hadn't done much more than peck me on the cheek for the last fifteen months of our marriage. At first, I'd assumed *I* was the problem, that he wasn't attracted to me anymore. My sense of style is a little more Doris Day than Marilyn Monroe, but I work out several days a week and take care of my body, which is more than he did. Then, I'd thought that it was him—as Emma got older and we got busier, he'd gained weight and struggled to keep up the last few times we did have sex. If it wasn't quick, he wasn't going to make it to the end, so sex had become a race to finish. Which had only been satisfying for one of us.

When I found out about his affair, I'd been relieved that I had a clear reason to get a divorce.

Combine that with the stress of moving into the shoebox apartment that was all I could afford, and I just didn't feel sexy.

I pull the lipstick vibrator out of the bag, turning it over in my hand. Now that I'm not on display to my coworkers and my fucking *boss*, I take my time examining it, noting that it's waterproof. I wouldn't admit it to Lauren at the time, but the design is clever. I've never owned a vibrator before. Jake and I were college sweethearts who got married our junior year when I found out I was pregnant with Emma. Vanilla sex is practically tattooed on our foreheads.

Not that I wouldn't have been open to trying something new, if he'd asked.

I pull the gold ring out next, sliding it onto my finger. I have to admit, it's pretty genius. I don't know if I'll ever be brave enough to wear it in public—Lauren tried to convince me to wear it last night, but I flat-out refused. Still, the idea of wearing it, knowing what it does, starts a low burning in my core.

What if I *did* wear it to work?

Writing forgotten, I lean back on the bathroom counter, tapping the button to turn on the ring. I picture myself sitting at my desk, typing up a memo, or answering the phone. It would be in that golden hour every afternoon, when everyone is back from lunch, and I have a blessed moment with no one asking me for help. I could easily slip the ring to the underside of my hand and slide it along one leg.

Slipping a hand under my skirt, it would be easy to glide the vibrating ring up my inner thigh, whispering it across my neglected clit.

A real gasp escapes me as I touch the ring to the sensitive skin of my thigh, the fabric of my leggings keeping the sensations muted. I'm aching for more.

I pull off my pants, tossing them on the floor, and lean back, running the vibrating ring up and down my thigh, enjoying the tingle of it. The vibration isn't intense but just enough to tease, to fill me with a need for more. A feeling I thought I'd forgotten.

That's a lie.

I felt it last night in the limo, Sutton stoking a fire deep in my being.

I let my mind wander back to doing this at work. The only way I would be caught is if someone stood directly over my desk, watching me from over the edge.

Only one person looms like that. Only one person in the building has that kind of presence.

Theo.

I gasp again as the vibrator taps near my clit, the thought of those glowering dark eyes watching me turning the low heat in my belly to a raging fire.

Would he stare like he did this afternoon? Would he drink in the sight of me touching myself at work? Would he bark at me like he does everyone else? I've never been on the receiving end of his wrath before this afternoon. Would it be hot? Or terrifying? Would I wilt under his gaze or would it make me bold?

Imaginary Sophie is much braver than real-life Sophie. In my mind, I'd know he was there, know he was watching me, and I wouldn't stop. I'd lean back in my chair, turning slightly to give him a better view of my hand disappearing under the fabric of my dress.

The vibrator hums nearer to where I need it, but I don't let it touch—teasing myself as much as I tease Sutton in my imagination.

Lazily, I let my hand slide up under my tank top, my fingers grazing my skin the way his eyes would trace a path along my body. I'm wet at the thought of him standing there, those dark eyebrows furrowed, hands in his pockets. Not saying anything, not stopping me, just watching.

Shit. The bathtub.

Turning off the ring, I toss it on the counter before reaching over to stop the water. Steam curls in the air, the mirror slightly fogged, obscuring me from the reality of looking at myself, allowing me to continue my fantasy.

I strip out of my clothes and am about to climb in when I pause. In a moment of desperation, I snatch the lipstick vibrator up and bring it with me, stepping into the scalding hot water before I can talk myself out of it.

It's research. I need to be able to do my characters justice. Jessie and Cody deserve good sex. If I have to lay in the bathtub and give myself an orgasm or two in order to do that, it's a sacrifice I'm willing to make.

The heat of the bath seeps into my bones as I lay back, eyes closed against the harsh light, fingers trailing lazy paths along my skin. Images of Sutton invade my mind, the same way his tongue invaded my mouth. If he'd known it was really me, not the mysterious Elinor Price, would he have kissed me last night?

I let myself imagine my hands are his, claiming every inch of me, hearing his growled words from the dark limo in my mind.

Use me.

My fingers pinch one nipple, while my other hand slides between my legs. I circle my clit, slow and steady.

I want to touch you.

I keep touching myself, a steady desire pulsing through me, building with each stroke.

I want to feel you come on my fingers.

I slide a finger inside myself. My orgasm creeps closer, an ache building up in my chest. For a second, I worry that I'm going to lose it, that I'll end up chasing it and getting nowhere just like the other night. I grab the lipstick vibrator with my free hand and flick it on, determined to find it.

A splash of hot water lands on my neck and I whimper, reminded of Theo's burning kisses along my jaw. The way he handled me, angling my head and neck exactly where he wanted them. I'd been relaxed, trusting him to take care of me in a way I haven't let anyone in a long time. If I'd let him, Theo would have instructed my body just like one of his brilliant programs—he would have brought me to orgasm with devastating precision.

I touch the vibrator to my thigh again, not sure what I want from it. What would Theo do? Would he take it from me with a growl? He would. He'd rip it from my lax fingers, impatient with my indecision and tell me to let him do it. With a quiet moan, I trace the vibrator along my center, one finger still working its way in and out.

Just thinking about Theo taking control, my mind releases the constant pressure of being on guard. With it, my orgasm inches closer.

I don't care about anything else, I just need you right now.

I bring the vibrator to my clit, remembering the desperation in Theo's tone, the way he'd looked deep into my eyes as the words had been ripped from him. My toes curl and the low burning in my core turns into an inferno. My stomach clenches and for a moment I forget how to breathe. Then my orgasm explodes through me and everything goes white. Trembling, I sink down into the water, boneless.

Oh my God.

A pink flush creeps over my skin and it's not from the heat of the water or the mind-blowingly intense orgasm I just had.

I just masturbated to thoughts of Theodore Sutton. The Bastard-in-Chief. My boss. And it was the best orgasm I've had in years.

Eleven

THEO

I'D NEVER TELL MY sister, but I secretly love the coffee warmer she had my niece give me for Christmas last year. I would happily tell my niece, but since Clara was only six months old at the time, I'm pretty sure she didn't do much in the way of picking it out.

The mug on top of it though, was decorated by my nephew Ethan, the splotches of color that I'm told are supposed to be me and Max, the height of five-year-old artistic endeavor. It's my favorite mug, but I only use it at home, preferring not to remind anyone in my office that I'm anything other than their boss.

I sip my coffee and stare at the lines of code in front of me. Another email vies for my attention, but I ignore it. Reading through the lines on my screen, I follow the path my brain created, looking for mistakes. Yet another email pops up in my peripheral vision as my cell phone rings with an incoming call.

"This is Sutton." I put the call on speaker, never taking my eyes off my screen, and wait for whoever's on the end of the line to speak.

"Mr. Sutton, it's five-thirty. I'm heading home and you should stop working for the day." I catch the sound of Mercedes' desk drawer opening and closing as she speaks. "Are you coming into the office tomorrow? I have some people waiting for an appointment with you."

I haven't been to the office all week. Determined to put Sophie out of my mind, I walked in on Monday morning, ready for another day of people not meeting my expectations and was completely undone by the cheerful "Good morning, Mr. Sutton," Sophie called out.

Logically, I know she's pretending that it wasn't her lips I devoured, or whose soft curves have haunted my dreams. She doesn't know that I know she's playing at being Elinor Price, but her easy smile and greeting was a knife to my gut. I lasted until lunchtime before running away. If I'd stayed, I would either have demanded to know what was so repulsive about me, or dragged her into my office for a do-over. The way she's invaded my mind is as irritating as it is illogical.

So I resorted to avoidance rather than facing her.

"I'll be in on Monday." I'll give myself the weekend to get my act together.

"Okay, sir. I'll make a note. Mr. Edwards' assistant has called twice trying to make an appointment with you this week. Something about a charity golf tournament next month."

I groan. "Dammit, Morgan knows I hate golf. Don't worry, I'll give him a call this weekend." I pause. "Tomorrow is Friday, right?"

"Yes it is." The humor in Mercedes's voice is audible even through the phone. "Coffee and donuts go to the third floor this week. It's already set up for delivery."

"You're the best, Mercedes." A smile tugs at the corner of my cheek. "What would I do without you?"

"Have to arrange a last-minute delivery of coffee and donuts to a different floor each week on your own?" Her teasing tone gets a real chuckle from me.

"Can you have them deliver an extra half dozen and coffees for the ladies at the front desk." I think for a second. "And Julian?"

"I'll do that now. Anything else?"

"No, I think that's everything. Goodnight, Mercedes."

"Goodnight, Mr. Sutton."

I wonder how Sophie takes her coffee? I know she drinks it, I've seen the odd mug by her keyboard—smelled the fresh scent of it as I've walked by her desk some mornings. Part of me wants desperately to know, but a bigger part of me is glad I don't—the temptation to have it sent to her would be more than I could resist.

That temptation is exactly why I left the office and haven't been back since. I don't trust myself not to pull Sophie into the elevator with me, press the emergency stop, and demand she tell me why she stopped us in the limo.

The woman is slowly driving me mad. And she doesn't have a clue.

I wrap up what I'm doing and close down my laptop for the evening. Contrary to popular belief, I don't work at all hours of the night. Once I'm done for the day, I'm done. "Max!" I head to my bedroom to change. "Wanna go for a run?"

"Max!" My voice carries down the deserted street. "Come here boy!" I try again.

I curse the stupid SUV full of teenagers that nearly ran us over. I'd jerked backwards when they came flying around the corner as Max and I stepped out into the crosswalk. Unfortunately, I'd hit the curb behind me and fallen flat on my ass, letting go of Max's leash in the process. By the time I'd managed to get to my feet, he'd been out of sight.

"Max! Here boy!" I keep calling as I wander up and down the streets, but no sign of Max. The farther I get from my street, the smaller and more run down the houses become. I start to circle back, intending to go home and see if Max was smart enough to sniff it out, when I hear someone else calling his name from the other end of the road.

"Max!" A high, feminine voice calls. "Max, where are you?"

Did someone hear me calling for my dog and decide to help me out? I jog down the street to see what's going on and stumble to a stop at the sight that meets my eyes. The blonde teenager whose cat got lost at the dog park the other week is wandering up and down the sidewalk in front of an apartment complex that's seen better days. The grass and planters in front of it are well-maintained, but the building could use a new coat of paint and repairs to the sagging banisters and stairwells.

"Uh, hi?' The girl eyes me warily. "Can I help you?"

"I lost my dog, Max. I heard someone calling him and came to see." I hold my hands up, not wanting to spook her.

"Your dog? I was calling my cat." Her shoulders slump in defeat as she realizes that I don't have her cat. "Wait, aren't you the guy from the dog park?"

"That's me. I haven't seen your cat, but I'll keep an eye out for him while I look for my dog. Let me know if you see him?" I step away to keep looking for my Max but she stops me, holding out one hand awkwardly.

"I'm Emma. Thanks for helping me look"

"Teddy." I'm not sure why I don't say Theo or Theodore, but the kid reminds me a little bit of Casey—all sass and confidence. I give her hand a firm shake. "I live a few streets over."

"In the really nice houses?" Her face changes at my nod. Her eyebrow game is strong, one lifting almost up to her hairline while the other stays perfectly still. "I live here." She jerks a thumb over her shoulder at the apartment building. "Um...do you remember what my cat looks like?"

"One ear, one eye? Mean little fuc—I mean, grumpy little guy?" I cough to cover up my almost curse.

"He's a mean little fucker, you can say it." Emma grins. "Don't tell my mom I said that."

I can't help laughing at her expression. "I won't tell." I promise her. "I'm going to go back this way, I'll let you know if I find your Max."

"Wait!" Emma's cry stops me before I've gone more than a few steps. "Let me give you my phone number. Um, Max is really my mom's friend's cat and has her number on his collar."

"And you weren't supposed to have him outside?" I raise an eyebrow at her but she doesn't cower from my glare the same way my employees do. Probably because I'm wearing athletic shorts and a t-shirt instead of a suit. "Let me guess, you were making a TikTok?"

Emma huffs and pouts for a second, before shrugging. "I won't tell my mom I keep running into this creepy old dude, if you don't tell her I lost the cat." Her face goes from thoughtful to smug by the end of her sentence.

"I'm not old!" I fight to keep a straight face as I say it, Emma's grin matching my own.

"You're not denying being creepy though."

"Denying it only makes it true." I shrug with a grin. "But I won't say anything about losing the cat. It's not like I know your mom anyways." I lie.

She holds out a hand and I give her my phone. She types for a second before the phone in her pocket buzzes. "Got it. I just texted myself from your phone. Good luck finding your Max!" I take back my phone before she whirls away, already calling for her cat.

Twenty minutes of wandering the streets later and I'm ready to give up. Praying he found his way home, I turn back onto my street. I'm passing under a tree when a pissed-off "meow" filters down from the branches overhead. Of course. A glance up confirms that the one-eyed, one-eared, son-of-a-whatever-you-call-a-female-cat, is perched above me, fur raised and spitting mad.

"For fuck's sake. Why are you always climbing trees if you can't get down?"

Max hisses at me, crouching down against the branch.

"Come here you idiot cat." Unlike at the dog park, I grab him from behind instead of where his sharp teeth and claws can get me again. Despite his squirming and wriggling, I manage to pull him off the branch and tuck him under my arm like a football.

Max the cat and I make it to my front door only slightly more ruffled than before, despite his attempts to escape my grasp. As soon as we're inside, I set him on the floor and pull out my phone.

Me: *Found your Max. I have him here at my house.*

I send my address and pace the entrance hall while I wait for a response. Max still isn't here and panic that he's been hurt claws at my chest. I need Emma to come get her cat quickly so I can go back to looking for him. What am I going to do if I can't find him? I'm not sure I'll be able to sleep tonight without his weight on my legs.

Emma: *We'll be there in 10 minutes. Driving over so we have the cat carrier.*

"Your people are on their way. Do not disappear." I point to my own eyes, then at Max the cat as he waddles down the hallway towards my kitchen. "And don't pee on my floor."

For the next ten minutes I trail along after the cat, determined not to let him out of my sight, ready to scoop him up and dump him in Emma's hands before going back to look for Max the second I can. I have to find him before it gets dark.

A buzz from my phone, a chime from my laptop, and the ringing of the doorbell all happen at once, my security systems doing their job of alerting me to someone at my door. I sweep Max up in one arm, before he can disappear on me, and head to the door.

"Here you go—" The words are barely out of my mouth before my Max barrels into my legs, jumping up to lick at my face. "Max, get down!" I shove at him with my free hand, juggling Max the cat in my other arm. Struggling to keep my footing and not drop the cat, I'm about to go down like an overloaded server when a pair of hands plucks the cat from my grip.

Shoving my Max behind me and into the house, I glare at him. "Sit. Stay." I don't turn my back on him until I'm sure he's going to do as I commanded before whirling back to face Emma.

I nearly swallow my tongue at the sight of Sophie Alexander standing on my doorstep, her curves highlighted by the leggings and loose tank top she's wearing, her hair golden in the light of the setting sun.

"M-Mr. Sutton?" Sophie's gasp sends the blood rushing away from my head. "Did you...how did...what?"

"I, uh..." My tongue gets stuck in my throat and I have to swallow hard before I can speak. "I met Emma at the dog park a few weeks ago. I just happened to run into her again while I was out looking for Max." I assumed Emma would drive herself over, I hadn't been prepared to come face-to-face with the reason I've been avoiding the office.

Sophie turns to look over her shoulder at a cowed Emma, before snapping her eyes back to me. "I had no idea, Mr. Sutton. I'm so sorry. I swear, I didn't know you lived here. It won't happen again. Thank you for finding the cat. We're going to go. *Now*." Sophie finally draws a breath as she hikes the cat against her shoulder and backs away, grabbing Emma by the shoulder.

Shit.

"Sophie." Her name is sunshine in my mouth, warming me up from the inside out. "Wait...please."

The scrabble of Max's claws against the wood floor of my house warns me to either go inside or close the door before he bolts again. "Would you like to come in for a moment?"

Sophie gapes at me, clutching the cat to her chest. Emma is the one who charges up the front steps and past me into the house. "Come on, Mom. Hi, Maxxy boy!"

Mom.

I knew that from seeing them at the dog park, but seeing them together drives it home.

Emma is *Sophie's* kid.

"Are you sure?" Sophie's question is so quiet I almost miss it.

"Moooooooom, Teddy invited you inside." Emma's impatience pulls a smirk from me. I step aside and wave Sophie into my house with a tip of my head. I don't know why I do, only a select few people have ever been inside.

From the outside, my home looks like a run-of-the-mill, solidly upper middle class home. Sure, five bedrooms is a little large for just me and Max, but when Casey and her family come to visit, we all enjoy that I have space enough for everyone to stay with me rather than a hotel.

Inside, I let my tech-loving nerd heart have free reign. If it can be controlled from an app, I probably have it built into my home. My sister convinced me to let her interior designer decorate the place for me, and my housekeeper Nan makes sure I never have to worry about anything but keeping it tidy between her visits. Could I live in a penthouse downtown with daily maid service and someone to take care of Max whenever I needed? Absolutely. Do I want to? Never.

"Teddy?" Sophie stops in front of me, one eyebrow quirked, her head tipped to the side. One sneakered foot taps a rhythm on my front porch. "No one calls you...Teddy."

My home is my sanctuary, my escape from being "Theodore Sutton, tech billionaire and most eligible bachelor in Portland." Once I walk through my front door I'm just Teddy. Although I didn't say no to the luxury of a five-head shower when Casey insisted it be installed. My older sister may have much more expensive taste than me, but she made my home a hidden oasis of luxury and I'm not complaining.

It takes everything in me not to kiss the incredulous look off Sophie's face. Instead I rub one hand on the back of my neck and shrug. "My sister does. I'm not always your scary boss, you know."

We stare at each other for a long minute, my eyes searching hers like in the dark of the limo. I don't want to tell her that I know she's Elinor Price, but I won't be mad if she admits it. Instead of slamming her lips against mine like she did after the gala, Sophie blinks and steps back, giving herself a small shake. "Thank you for finding the cat, but we can't impose on your weekend." She leans into the house. "Emma, come on. Let's go!"

"But Mom, have you seen his backyard? It's huge!" Emma's voice drifts back to us.

Sophie closes her eyes briefly, before startling me by bellowing into my house. "Emma Grace Miller, quit stalling and get your ass out here right now." Her blue eyes go wide when she realizes what she said and one hand claps over her mouth. "Oh my God, I can't believe I just said that in front of you." Her cheeks turn scarlet when I chuckle.

And because I just can't help myself—I take a step closer and lean down to whisper in her ear. "I promise not to tell the Bastard-in-Chief. Your secret is safe with me." My lips brush her ear as I speak, her arms holding the cat pressing against my chest. All it would take is one more step for us to be pressed against each other, but I don't. I can't, no matter how much I want to.

Emma brushes past Sophie, knocking her forward that last inch. I steady her with my hands on her waist while Emma stomps down the steps to the sidewalk, oblivious to us. Sophie's breath hitches in her chest at the contact. Does she remember the way my fingers feel on her body the same way I do?

Twelve

SOPHIE

"I...WE SHOULD GO...I NEED to take her to...nevermind." I stutter over the words. Now that I've brought his dog back, I should retreat, but I make no attempt to walk away. Theo's fingers flex on my waist, holding me still.

Does he know that was me in the limo? Theo's hands on my body are thrilling and familiar in a way I don't understand. I should be running for the car right now. Hell, there's a lot of things I should be doing right now that would be way more appropriate for the boss/employee relationship we have.

His eyes hold mine captive and the world stops turning for a second. A car door opens and closes, probably Emma, but I don't look, too lost in the ocean-blue pools above me. Max squirms in my arms, reminding me why I'm here in the first place. I blink, breaking the spell between us, and step back.

"Thank you for finding Max." I lift the cat in thanks and start to turn away. "I'll see you on Monday?"

Theo's hand on my elbow stops me walking away. "Thank you. I'd be lost without my Max." He leans forward a fraction, as if he's going to step into my space again. Is he going to hug me? Kiss me?

Did I just turn into Keira Knightley in *Pride and Prejudice*? Is it raining?

But before anything interesting can happen, he straightens up. My mouth drops open, whether to speak or in shock I don't know, and Theo reaches out to close it. "Goodbye, Ms. Alexander, I'll see you on Monday."

I swear he caresses my jaw before dropping his hand, but he wouldn't. Would he?

My hot as an Arizona summer, cold as an Alaskan winter, and sexy as sin boss did not just run a finger along my jaw. And he definitely did not brush his thumb over my bottom lip. And he absolutely *did not* have a hard on when he was pressed against me in his doorway.

Heart racing, I escape to my car, the dinged-up paint on my ten-year-old Toyota sticking out like a sore thumb in this neighborhood full of Tesla's. Thankfully, Emma has the cat carrier open and ready for Max when I get there, even as her nose is buried in her phone. "Emma, put your phone away and help me." I wrestle Max into the carrier, ignoring his protests, then hold my hand out. "Phone. Now."

"But Mom!"

"Now." I take her phone and drop it in my purse behind me before starting the engine.

"He's staring."

I'm tempted to look, but I force myself to turn the key in the ignition with a little prayer that it starts on the first try. The last thing that I need is for my billionaire boss to see me struggle to start my car. "Why are you so bent out of shape, Mom? And how do you know him?"

Thank God it starts. I pull away from the curb with only one glance in the rear-view mirror. Mr. Sutton stands in his open doorway, watching me pull away. "That's my boss, Emma. He owns Mailbox."

"Oh shi—shoot. I didn't get you in trouble, did I?" Emma's teenage attitude melts away when she realizes exactly who that was.

She may be fifteen and full of sass, but she's not a bad kid at heart. Just impulsive.

I smack her leg. "Don't swear. And no, I'm not in trouble. But you are." Turning out of the upscale neighborhood, I remind myself to turn left toward Jake's new apartment, not right to go home. I use the moment to count to twenty before I speak. Emma doesn't know that was the single most embarrassing and arousing moment of my life. I'm not sure if I'm counting to stop myself from yelling at her, or because just that little bit of contact between us has me squeezing my thighs together.

"Mom."

I ignore her, concentrating on not crashing the car or turning around so I can throw myself at Theodore Sutton's dick.

"Mo-om." The whining in her tone matches the whining of my lady bits, all of which are screaming at me to turn this car around.

"Ugh!" Emma flops back in the seat next to me, crossing her arms and exuding teenage attitude from every pore of her slightly oily face.

"What?" I give in and ask as I merge onto the highway.

"Are you really going to make me spend the weekend with Dad *and* without my phone?" She sighs heavily, as only an adolescent girl can. "Isn't making me spend the weekend with Dad punishment enough?"

"Emma! He's your father. Spending time with him isn't a punishment."

"It is though," she mutters. "It's not like you're doing anything special. Why can't I stay home with you?"

Keeping my own sigh buried, I twist my hands on the steering wheel. "We have to stick to the custody arrangement we worked out with the mediator, sweetie. If I don't hold up my end of the bargain and make sure you see your dad, then he doesn't have to hold up his end of the bargain. It's only one weekend a month—you can manage." Not that Jake's paltry child support payments make much difference, but it's the principle of the thing. Besides, I'll be damned if Jake can blame their bad relationship on anyone but himself.

"Don't let Dad forget to take you to your appointment tomorrow morning. It's your annual check-up with Dr. Clark."

I hate that Emma's appointment with her doctor is on Jake's weekend, but he assured me that he would take her. In exchange, I get a weekend with the apartment to myself and the chance to sleep in the real bed instead of on the couch for two nights in a row. How sad is it that it's become the highlight of my month?

"Can I have my phone back?"

"You can have it back when I drop you off. For now, your punishment for losing Max, *again*, is that you have to, horror of horrors, have an actual conversation with your mother." I should be more upset about the cat incident, but Max is a slippery guy and I've accidentally let him out of the house more than once myself. I don't miss Emma's smirk and head shake at my idea of a punishment, even if she covers it with a scowl a second later.

Pulling up to Jake's apartment, I roll down the windows before I park. "Okay sweetie, try not to be too miserable." My tone is teasing but I mean the words sincerely. Emma and Jake had a pretty contentious relationship before he and I separated, and the divorce has only made it worse. But he fought for his weekends with her and I would never stand in the way of them seeing each other.

Emma grabs her bag from the backseat before wrapping her arms around me in a hug. "Bye Mom, love you. I'll do my best, but I make no promises."

She's halfway up the steps to his place when the door opens and my ex-husband steps out, face already pulled into a glower.

"What the fuck, Sophie? You guys were supposed to be here an hour ago."

With a glance back at me, Emma hesitates. "It's okay sweetie, go on inside. I'll see you on Sunday night." I wave her toward the door.

Jake thunders down the stairs toward me, his skin flushed an unattractive red, but I ignore him until Emma is inside and the door is shut behind her. "I sent you a text, Jake. The cat got out and we were looking for him. Can you not yell at me in front of her?"

"I'm not yelling at you." He cuts me off before I can say anything snarky in response. "This weekend is important to me, whether you think it is or not. She's my daughter too."

I roll my eyes. "You're raising your voice at me—last time I checked, that fits the definition of yelling. I know she's your daughter too—I was there when it happened." Do I confront him about what I know? Or wait until he says something? Do I even want to have this conversation right now? No, I don't. I want to leave before I have to talk to him any longer. I swear to God if he tries to tell me about his new fiancée, I will lose my mind right here in the parking lot. "Whatever. I'll see you on Sunday."

"Sophie..."

"What?"

"Nevermind. See you Sunday."

And that right there is probably half the reason we're divorced, apart from the cheating and the lying. For all my snark, I'm terrified of confrontation and would rather pretend to be ignorant than have a hard conversation. Communicating through my writing I can do, but communicating my feelings? I'd rather have a root canal.

I slink back to my car and head home, waving to Emma through the window before I pull out.

I'd rather choke on the words I want to say than fight. If I hadn't caught him cheating red-handed, who knows if I ever would have had the guts to leave him. I'd resigned myself to a lifetime of suffering in silence, never telling him how I felt.

His reckless spending, inability to keep a job, constant complaining and general negative attitude never felt like reason enough to leave him. So I'd swallowed it down and sentenced myself to death by a thousand cuts. Even Lauren had almost lost patience with me over it, pushing me to speak up for myself before it was too late.

Lauren is out of town this weekend, so I head home alone, no reason to go anywhere else. "Come on Max, no more running away okay? And definitely no more running into Mr. Sutton."

Had he really told Emma his name was Teddy? I can't reconcile the stern Theodore I know from the office, or the sexy and suave Theo from the gala, with *Teddy*. Teddy Sutton. I can't wrap my brain around it. Maybe I read *Little Women* too many times as a kid, but Teddy makes me think of a happy-go-lucky man-child who's never faced a hardship greater than being rejected by a girl.

But Theo? Just the thought of Theo Sutton—of the way his stubble scraped my skin, the tickle of his breath against my ear, his hands burning into my skin—has heat building in my core and my clit aching for relief.

Driving home is torture, the need in my belly burning brighter and brighter with each memory I relive. Flashes from the limo ride haunt me as I park at home. One look at my apartment is like a bucket of cold water being thrown at me. His world and mine will never come together—the billionaire and the secretary? I cringe at the cliche, pulling Max out of the backseat.

Instead of taking care of the need still burning low in my belly, I lock the door behind me, let Max out of his carrier, and pour myself a glass of wine before pulling out my laptop.

Jessie and Cody are about to benefit from the pent up sexual tension Theo Sutton sent racing through me. If I can't work this tension out myself, I'll work it out through my words. I resigned myself to being the stereotypical 'frustrated housewife reading romance novels because she's not getting any from her husband' years ago. Now I'm a divorced, single mom in my mid-thirties who has an unbearable crush on her boss. Just trading one stereotype for another.

Jessie and Cody work out their differences with a lot of tongue action, both dialogue and other, more interesting uses. In my mind, though, it's Theo doing these things to my body.

By the time I've drunk two glasses of wine and written Jessie her third orgasm, my panties are soaked and I've done enough Kegels to keep my bladder in good shape until I die. If I don't do something about this soon, I'm going to do something stupid. Like text my boss.

Because I saved his number off his dog's collar and didn't delete it the second I realized whose number it was, like I should have.

Maybe it's the wine, maybe it's the lava-hot scene I just wrote, but the temptation is more than I can bear. He was flirting with me, right? I didn't imagine the way he looked at me, did I? Like he was starving and I was a feast.

My phone is in my hand and my fingers are typing before I can stop myself.

Me: If you weren't my scary boss...

I can't think of how I want to finish that sentence. If you weren't my boss, I'd send you a picture of my boobs? An answering text comes in a moment later.

Other Max: If I wasn't your scary boss what? Would I be curious why the beautiful woman who rescued my dog is texting me late on a Friday night?

I debate changing his name in my contacts. For my own sanity, I can't use his real name. I grin as I change it, then bite my bottom lip while I try to think of a response. I'm pretty sure my brain short-circuited when he called me beautiful.

Tall, Dark & Handsome: If I WAS your boss, I would be annoyed that it's taking this long to get a response from my employee. But since I'm pretending that's not the case, I suppose I have to be patient.

This is followed by a gif of Inigo Montoya saying "I hate waiting." The giggle that sounds in my empty apartment is definitely from the wine, not because my grumpy boss just sent me a silly gif. Theodore Sutton and The Princess Bride do not go together.

> **Me:** *There's no way this is my boss. My scary boss, who walks into the office every day yelling at someone new, would never be caught dead sending a gif from The Princess Bride.*

> **Tall, Dark & Handsome:** *Theodore Sutton's favorite movie is The Godfather II—I'm sure I read it in an article somewhere, so it must be true. But Teddy's favorite movie is The Princess Bride. It's a classic.*

Oh. My. God. There is a winky face emoji in that text. Have I entered the Twilight Zone? I curl my legs up under me on the couch, laptop forgotten on the coffee table.

> **Me:** *Have you been kidnapped? Is there a ransom note? Do I need to send help? Is there someone in the FBI I should contact? How do I know I'm not texting with a kidnapper?*

> **Tall, Dark & Handsome:** *I'm not a kidnapper.*

I wonder where Theo is in that giant house. Is he lounging on the leather couch I caught a glimpse of through the door? Or was he working at his desk and I interrupted him? I stop myself before I imagine him lying in bed and texting me, it's too dangerous to let my mind wander that direction.

Me: That's what a kidnapper would say.

Me: Besides, I'm not even sure that really was my scary boss who rescued my cat. I've never seen my boss wearing anything other than a suit and tie. The man who had my cat was wearing a t-shirt and shorts, which I'm not convinced my boss owns.

The tailored suits he wears at work have always hugged his toned body, but seeing him dressed so casually had done something unholy to my insides.

Tall, Dark & Handsome: *Sophie...*

A shiver runs down my spine as I imagine him saying my name. The exasperated growl I imagine he'd finish with.

Me: Yes?

Tall, Dark & Handsome: *Why did you text me?*

Me: Honestly?

Me: I don't know.

Tall, Dark & Handsome: *Let me know when you figure it out.*

Thirteen

THEO

YOU KNOW WHAT'S WORSE than being woken up by your famous sister and her equally-famous husband video calling you at five in the morning on a Saturday?

Being woken up by the celebrity duo video chatting you from Bora Bora while sporting the hard-on from hell, and not being awake enough to realize they can see it.

"Yo, Teddy, put that weapon away!" Garrett laughs at me.

"Did we wake you up? Sorry!" Casey's face leaning over Garrett's shoulder is deeply tanned and fresh. "We just wanted to say hi. I guess I got the time difference wrong. We haven't gone to bed yet."

I push myself up out of bed, careful not to wake up the snoring Max next to me. "I don't want to know why you're still awake, isn't it two in the morning for you? My alarm would have gone off in a few minutes anyways. But that's what you get for waking me up." I take the phone with me to the kitchen so I can make coffee. "How's the tropical life?"

Casey and Garrett fill me in on their adventures—snorkeling and lounging in their private bungalow. "Why are you awake, anyways?" I ask before jealousy eats too far into my stomach lining.

"That's my fault." Garrett's grin is easy

"Ahhh, yes, the vampire movie is up next, right? Trying to prepare for all those night shoots, huh?"

Casey blushes and Garrett grins.

"Never mind, I don't want to know."

"Probably for the best. So what, or should I say who, has you waking up in such a state?" Garrett pulls the phone from Casey. "Go away babe, Teddy and I need to have a big brother chat."

Cringing, I sip my coffee. "I'm fine."

"No you're not, Teddy. I can tell. Besides, you've only emailed us once this week. So, who's got you distracted?"

Should I tell him? Who else would I tell? My brother-in-law is the closest thing to a friend I have at this point. Growing up in Casey Sutton's shadow with the ultimate stage mom didn't make it easy for me to make friends. Especially when I turned out to be more kid-genius than child star. My mom was so busy managing Casey's career, and sleeping with Casey's agent, and stealing Casey's money, that she didn't have much time for me. When our mom and Casey's former agent concocted a scandal about Garrett and Casey having some kind of under-age affair, my sister and I both cut ties with her.

"It's my admin."

"Mercedes? Isn't she old enough to be your mother?"

I choke on my coffee. "No, God no. I meant the one who sits at the main reception desk. You probably don't remember her."

"The blonde? I remember her. She was super sweet and kept an eye on Ethan while I changed Clara's diaper last time we were there. What about her?" His voice drops down to a whisper. "I mean, she's very attractive, but why now? She's been there for years hasn't she?"

"Three, to be exact."

"Damn, bro, you've been keeping track?" There's rustling over the line and the faint sound of waves gets louder. "Tell me more."

I fill Garrett in on the situation, how I found out about her divorce, how she'd shown up as Elinor Price. Then I tell him about the night of the gala.

"So she showed up in a hot dress and glasses, pretending to be this Elinor Price chick, and made out with you in the limo on the way home? But then she flipped a switch and gave you the cold shoulder? What happened now, because none of this explains why you're uncharacteristically worked up."

"Long story short, I lost Max, she lost her cat. I found her cat and she found my dog. I didn't know it was her cat until she showed up to get him and then...Garrett, I swear if her kid hadn't been there, I would have hauled her into the house and fucked her against the door right then and there. How is she doing this to me, man?"

Garrett's laugh is long and loud. Loud enough that Casey pops up on the screen. "What am I missing?" Between bouts of laughter, Garrett catches her up while I finish my coffee

When he's finished, I add the missing information explaining why they woke me up in the middle of the hottest dream I've ever had, with a dick hard enough to play a game of baseball. "She ended up with my number, from Max's tag I assume, and was, uh, texting me last night."

"Theodore Sebastian Sutton, tell me you did *not* sext your receptionist last night!" There's a flurry of activity and the camera whirls wildly before landing facing the dark sky. I can hear Casey and Garrett laughing and exclaiming for a minute before Garrett picks up the phone.

"Sorry, Casey almost fell off the deck in her shock. I had to rescue her." His smirk is all I need to convince me I do not want him to give me any more details.

I pull a yogurt out of my fridge and pop the top off. "No Casey. I did not *sext* the secretary—that sounds like terrible porn, by the way—*she* flirted with *me*."

"Define flirting." Casey's voice floats up from somewhere behind the camera. "Were any naughty words used?"

"No. But there may have been a Princess Bride gif and an emoji." I cringe, knowing Casey is going to catch onto it immediately.

"No!" Her face fills the screen when she steals the phone from Garrett. "Princess Bride? I thought only I was special enough to get Princess Bride gifs from you!"

I don't say anything, just shrug.

"Babe, he really likes her." Garrett's face squishes back onto the screen. "Okay, so what's the problem?" Casey's question is what kept me up half the night.

"I'm the fucking CEO."

"So? She's not your immediate subordinate, right? You don't actually manage her at work do you? Don't you just walk past her pretending to be on your phone and yelling at podcast hosts? Take her on a date. See what happens."

Me: *How do you feel about cheese danishes?*

Sunshine: *Besides the fact that they are the perfect breakfast pastry?*

Me: *I'm at The Beanery around the corner from the dog park and they happen to make an excellent cheese danish here.*

Sunshine: *Are you asking me to meet you at The Beanery?*

Me: *I'm offering to buy you one, and coffee too if you want it. If you want to meet me here.*

Sunshine: *Is this work related?*

Me: *No.*

Sunshine: *Is this a date?*

"Is it a date, Max?" He just looks at me with big brown eyes. "You're not helpful."

Me: *This is me, Teddy, asking you, Sophie, to meet me for coffee at an establishment that I believe is a convenient distance from both our homes. Because I would enjoy having your company this morning, and I'm hoping you are open to the idea of seeing me outside of work hours and for non work-related activities.*

Sunshine: *You could have just said yes.*

Me: *Yes.*

Me: *Better?*

Sunshine: *I'll be there in five minutes. I expect a cheese danish and a mocha waiting for me when I arrive.*

I spend those five minutes ordering her drink and pacing. Max follows me as I pace from one end of the sidewalk to the other, his tongue hanging out of his mouth. July in Portland isn't hot the way July in Los Angeles is, but it's hot enough.

Five minutes later, Sophie appears around the corner. She's wearing a blue sundress that I've never seen her wear to the office, probably because of the way it dips down low between her perfect breasts. The yellow sandals on her feet are sensible but cute. My heart twists at the sight of her. My dick gives a hopeful little twitch too.

Holding out the paper cup with her drink, I smile at the wary expression on her face.

"Good morning." Her words are laced with uncertainty. If she's hoping I have any idea what I'm doing, she's going to be disappointed.

"Morning." I fumble with the end of Max's leash. "Did you sleep okay?"

Sophie stares at me, her eyebrows drawn together, a cute little wrinkle forming between them. "Did you just...did you really just ask me if I *slept okay*? Who are you?" Before I can answer, she holds up a hand, stalling me. "Sorry, don't answer that. That was rude. I'm just..."

"Flustered? Confused? Completely unsure of what to say or do next? Worried you're going to say something to upset me?" I offer. Sophie nods and I shrug. "Me too." Again, I offer her the paper cup that she still hasn't taken from me.

This time she takes it, her fingers brushing mine, before retreating a couple steps. I suppress my need to pull her close at just that little bit of contact. "Yeah, but you invited me here. You didn't have a plan? You're—" she waves a hand up and down my body. "I assumed you had a master plan."

We're still standing an awkward distance apart in front of the coffee shop, Max sniffing hopefully around the legs of the table next to me. I take a sip of my latte to stall for time. Sophie mirrors me by taking a sip of her drink. Her eyes close for a moment while she swallows, savoring the sip with a hum. That hum sends a little more blood away from my brain and I rock on my heels to shake it off.

"I told you, today I'm just Teddy."

Sophie cocks her head to the side, eyeing me. "Just Teddy?"

I hold out the cheese danish I got for her, paper bag rustling with either the breeze or my shaking hand. Sophie takes it, looking around. "Well, Just Teddy, did you want to sit down or...?"

I point at Max. "I was thinking maybe we could take him to the dog park?" I pray that Sophie will go along with it, trusting in my favorite play of "fake it till you make it" to get past the awkwardness. *I* know we've already been out together once. *I* know what her lips taste like, how easy she is to be around. And I know she knows some of that about me too, but she doesn't know that I know. And I'm going to tell her, just...not yet. For some reason, it feels like something I need to tell her face to face, not over the phone, and not when I'm looming over her at work.

With Max leading the way, we stroll in the direction of the dog park, the same one where I met Emma. We make it half a block before Sophie speaks. When she does, the questions pour out of her.

"I'm so confused, Mr. Sutton. I don't understand why I'm here. I know you said it's not work-related. I don't need a thank-you coffee, or whatever this is, for finding your dog. Anyone would have done the same. And if this is because of the text I sent last night, I'm sorry. I realize it was probably inappropriate. I'd had a couple glasses of wine and...I don't really know why I texted you, or what the point was. I was just..."

She trails off, inhaling deeply. "Lonely?" I offer up the word with a smile before taking a sip of my drink.

Sophie stops walking, turning to face me. "Why me?"

Instead of answering her, I keep walking down the street, letting her catch up. "You know I don't date, right?" I glance down at her, catching the way the sunshine paints her golden hair as she nods. "The other night, I was supposed to attend a fundraiser with my sister, but since her husband whisked her away on a last-minute vacation, I found myself dateless."

"Would that be such a bad thing?"

I shrug. "Personally, I don't care. But any time I show up at an event like that Morgan—" I catch myself before I give away that I know she met him. "My mentor will use it as an excuse to set me up with one of his many nieces, cousins, grandkids, or various hangers-on."

"I take it you don't care for the kinds of girls he sends your way?" She's picking at the paper sleeve of her cup. Is she nervous? Has she figured out that I know she's Elinor?

"No. I prefer to spend my time with people I can have an intelligent conversation with."

"Oh." Her response is so quiet I almost miss it.

The gated fence to the dog park on my right has Max tugging on the leash. I pause my story to open the gates and let us all in before unclipping him. He takes off at a sprint around the space, like he always does, and I pull Sophie by the elbow into the shade of the same tree her Max got stuck in.

Her blue eyes are wide as I look into them, her bottom lip caught between her teeth. "Imagine my surprise when I had Ms. Masterson arrange for Elinor Price to accompany me and *you* showed up."

"I can explain..."

I shake my head. "No need, I know what a pen name is. What I don't understand is how you thought I wouldn't recognize you?"

Sophie doesn't answer, her eyes still searching mine. I take a chance on stepping closer, not enough to touch, but enough to let the warmth of her skin soak into me. I don't like the dejected look on her face, the way her teeth are worrying her lip. "Do you think I don't notice you because you're the receptionist?"

"Something like that, yeah."

"How could I *not* notice the one person in the whole company who looks me in the eye every day? Your first day at Mailbox you smiled at me and said 'good morning, sir' in that cheerful way you always do. Even when I walk in with the scowliest of scowls on my face, you smile at me."

A giggle escapes Sophie. "Did...did you just say 'scowliest of scowls'?" The giggles turn into a full-throated laugh. "Who are you and what have you done to the Theodore Sutton I know?"

Max comes nosing back to us, bumping his head against my leg. "Hang on boy, we have a situation here." I scratch the top of his head while Sophie belly laughs beside me. I hide my grin by roughing up Max's ears the way he loves. "I told you, today I'm Teddy."

"You say that like Teddy and Theodore are two different people. Should I be worried? Is Theo also a different personality?" Sophie manages to get out between giggles. I squat down to dig in Max's harness for the ball I stowed there earlier.

"If I said yes would you run away screaming? I have to be Theodore at work. Theodore has to make tough calls, be the hardass who gets things done. Teddy hates that kind of thing, just wants to play with code and hang out with his dog. Is that weird?"

Sophie squats down next to me to pet Max. "So, behind that scary front you put on at the office, you're just a sweet guy named Teddy who likes to play with computers and his dog?" She pauses, glancing at me. "I imagine being the CEO of a company like Mailbox is harder when everyone thinks you're easy to take advantage of. So the gruff armor protects your soft, squishy insides?"

Max punctuates her words with an impetuous lick of her chin. Sophie falls back with a laughing cry, her feet slipping out in front of her.

"Max!" I push him back before he can knock Sophie down again, although she's grinning and making no attempt to stand back up. I toss his ball as far across the grassy park as I can before sitting down next to her. My legs stretch out inches past hers, our shoulders bump softly as her laughter infects me.

"So, we've established that my multiple personalities are a defense mechanism at work. You know you can't tell anyone at the office about Teddy, right?"

Sophie mimes zipping her lips. I want to kiss those lips.

"What's with yours?" I have to know. Did she pretend to be Elinor for the same reason I pretend to be someone I'm not? "I understand the need for a pen name, but why not come clean at the fundraiser?"

The smile drops off Sophie's face at my questions. "Honestly? I just didn't want to be sad, old Sophie Alexander. Dressing up, going somewhere fancy? That's not my life. I felt like Cinderella. I just wanted to pretend to have a different life for a night. Elinor doesn't share a one-bedroom apartment with her teenage daughter and sleep on the couch, doesn't have to worry about paying the bills, or deal with her ex-husband." She shrugs and the weight of her life settles back on her shoulders. I hadn't even noticed the difference until it changed. I hate seeing her defeated, it makes all my protective instincts roar to life. "I wanted to apologize for my behavior that night, actually. I, uh, got some upsetting news right before you got there."

Max lopes back and drops his ball in my lap. I scoop it up and toss it for him again, giving Sophie a moment to gather her thoughts.

"As Lauren has loudly proclaimed to everyone in the office, you know I'm newly divorced, right?"

"I may have overheard your conversation at Uno, Dos, Tres on your birthday." I rub the back of my neck.

"Long, sad, story short, I found out right before you arrived that my ex-husband not only was cheating on me for longer than I thought, but he and his girlfriend just got engaged. And she's pregnant." Her breath whooshes out of her in a gust and she flops back in the grass. I'm torn between admiring the extra inches of her lean thigh the movement exposes and pulling her into my arms, while a murderous rage in my gut insists I need to do something about her ex. I let myself drink in her thighs for a moment before

I do the smarter thing and stretch out next to her, head propped up on my elbow.

"That would explain the throwing up and the shots of whiskey." I'd been judgmental of it, even though she hadn't seemed drunk at all. But now, hearing about the news she'd received just moments before? I'm in awe of her strength, that she was able to push aside something so upsetting to play nice and make small talk for hours. Not only that, but converse knowledgeably and sincerely with everyone we encountered.

Sophie groans, throwing an arm over her eyes. "Don't remind me. I was being such a cow that night."

"You were utterly charming." I reach out and pinch the ends of her fingers with mine, wiggling her arm lightly, hoping the silly gesture brings a smile to her face. "Well, to everyone except me." She doesn't move, but she does turn her head, looking at me from underneath her arm. Her small smile is tinged with sadness and something else.

Before I can ask what she's thinking, Max comes charging between us, tail wagging and paws dancing too close to Sophie's stomach. He drops the now slobbery ball on her chest and steps on the almost empty cup sitting next to me. Coffee and chocolate dregs explode everywhere, splattering both of us.

"I'm sorry." I reach out to shove Max out of the way, but my big dopey dog is too busy chasing his tail in the space between us. Laughing, Sophie sits up and tosses the ball for him, sending him running after it and giving us space to assess the damage.

We sit there for a second, just staring at each other. There's a drip of coffee running down Sophie's cheek, a Pollock-inspired splatter across the side of her dress and a decent-sized splash on the side of her arm. Her laughter dies as she takes in my damage—there's a trail of it tickling my neck, pooling against the collar of my shirt, and a hit of it decorating my chest.

I wonder if she wants to lick the drips off me the same way I want to lick them off her?

Fourteen

SOPHIE

ON A SCALE OF one to can-never-show-my-face-at-work-again, how inappropriate would it be to lean in and lick the trail of coffee running down Theo's neck? His eyes have gone dark, just like they did in the limo seconds before we kissed. I'd thought it was a trick of the light at the time, but maybe I was wrong.

Before I can decide how much I'm willing to humiliate myself, Theo leans forward and swipes the drop of coffee off my cheek. Without breaking eye contact, he sucks it off his finger. This isn't the disconcertingly playful Teddy anymore, lulling me into a sense of ease with his banter and "aw shucks'" charm. No. This is Theo. A predator. A man who knows how to get what he wants.

Me.

So of course I do the stupidest thing possible.

I lean forward and lick the coffee off his neck. I don't run away. I don't hop up and apologize or try to clean up the situation. And I don't just lick the droplet off. If I'm going to make things messy, I'm going to make things really messy, so I lick all the way from the collar of his shirt to that sharp jaw, before veering left and running my tongue all the way to his ear. I don't catch his earlobe between my teeth, though, because Theo grabs hold of the back of my neck and pulls me back with a feral growl.

Heat races up my chest and cheeks. "Oh my God…" I trail off when Theo doesn't yell at me. He's holding me captive, staring at me. I swallow. "Um…"

Before I can say anything else, Theo crashes his lips against mine. His kiss is hard, possessive, demanding. I can't help the tiny moan that escapes me as all the fun parts of my body light up. His tongue sweeps against mine and my hand curls against his chest, grabbing his shirt.

The wetness of his shirt and a whiff of doggy breath hit me at the same time, yanking me back to reality. I pull away from Theo with a gasp, my cheeks on fire. I scramble to my feet, common sense yelling at me that we're in public, that I'm his employee, and that there's no way a man like Sutton wants a nobody like me.

"Sophie."

I ignore his gruff voice, fumbling in my pocket, hunting for a tissue or a napkin.

"Sophie." His growl is closer. I ignore the way he says my name, with just a hint of pleading.

His hand grips my wrist. "Sophie. Stop."

I freeze, eyes down, until Theo's finger under my chin encourages me to look up. When I meet his eyes, all the air leaves my lungs. He's not angry. I know what angry Theo looks like and it's not this. "I can't believe I just did that." I whisper, mortification sweeping over me. He has a firm grip on my chin, his thumb millimeters from my bottom lip. The ghost of his touch shoots electricity through my veins.

"Can't believe you licked me? Or kissed me?" He takes a step closer, not letting go, not letting me look anywhere else. "It's not like we haven't kissed before, *Elinor*." His eyes drop to my lips before sliding back up to mine. "We should get cleaned up." There's a promise in his voice of something more than just cleaning up and it has my lady bits clamoring to find out what it is.

Without letting go of my wrist, Theo whistles for Max. "Do you promise not to run away this time?"

Run away? He must mean like I did after the fundraiser. "I promise." My skin is tingling with the promise in his eyes.

Theo lets go of my wrist to hook Max's leash on, then threads his fingers through mine. "Come on, my house is just around the corner."

My stomach full of butterflies, I follow Theo through the gate and down the street. The sun is on my skin, the drying coffee tickles my arm, and Theo's warm fingers hold mine.

My skin is aching for Theo to touch it. My lips burn to kiss him again. Is this what lust feels like? Like I'm going to explode if Theo looks at me with those hungry eyes again? Or like I'll wither away if he doesn't?

Has it really been so long since I've felt this that I've forgotten how consuming it is? I make sure not to dwell on the fact that this is a *terrible* idea. Fooling around with your boss is never a good idea, no matter how many romances I've read that say otherwise. This is only going to end in heartache and drama, but right now, I don't care.

Someone wants me.

June Cleaver, always has a pen in her purse, maternal me.

And it's not just anyone who wants me. The most eligible man in Portland. A man who grew up going to red carpet events with his older sister, who could have any woman he wanted. And he's choosing me.

If he never wants to see me again, and he probably won't, I'm going to revel in this moment. I'm going to store it away in my memory for a lonely night.

His house really is just around the corner, and it's a good thing. I'm wound so tight by the time we finish our silent walk that I think I might orgasm from just a word.

He pulls his phone out of his pocket as we walk up the steps, touching his thumb to a pad on the screen. There's a click and a beep from the front door as we stand in front of it. I swear he moves in slow motion, my body screaming at him to do something, or maybe that's just my neglected bits clearing out the cobwebs. Cracking open the door, Theo leans down to let Max off his leash before pulling me inside.

The door is barely closed before my back hits it, Theo's lips ravaging mine. His hands slide up my waist, pushing my arms up above my head. He holds my wrists with one hand, the other skimming down to grab my hips and pull himself closer. I'm pinned to the door by his hips, his hands, and his kiss and I love it. I luxuriate in the feeling of being wanted so desperately.

"Tell me to stop," Theo whispers against my skin as his lips leave mine, only to start kissing along my jaw. His hand on my hip kneads and pulls at me, bunching the fabric of my dress in his fingers.

"Don't...stop," I whimper. My hips writhe against the door and I tip my head to the side, giving him better access to my neck. "Whatever you do, don't stop."

With my last word, Theo lets go of my wrists, and I drop my arms over his shoulders, pulling him back to my lips. Sliding both hands to my thighs, Theo doesn't break our kiss as he picks me up. "You're the boss."

My grin at his words turns into a cry as my back hits the door again, this time with Theo's hard cock rubbing against my core. I wrap my legs around his hips, desperate for more friction.

He grinds against me as I claw at his back, tugging and pulling at his shirt. Frustrated that I can't get it off him, I break the kiss. "Lose your shirt."

"Maybe I don't want to put you down." Theo's hips keep grinding against me as he sucks and nibbles along my collarbones.

"I thought I was the boss."

"Did I say that?"

"You did." I tug at his shirt again. "Now—Lose. The. Shirt."

The delicious pressure of Theo's cock against me stops, but he doesn't put me down. "As you wish." Reaching back with one arm, he pulls his shirt over his head and drops it to the ground.

His chest is a work of art. My fingers dance over the chiseled muscle, brushing the sprinkle of hair that covers it. Everyone at the office knows he's in good shape, but the reality is so much better than I could have imagined. Theo kisses along my jaw as my fingers wander over the ridges of his abs. His lips vibrate against me with a groan as I sweep my hands around to his back, trailing my nails along his bare skin.

"Hey, boss?" Theo's words caress my skin.

"Yes?" I can't help grinning.

"I'd like to propose a horizontal collaboration between all parties involved."

I let out a sigh as Theo nibbles his way down the side of my neck. "I would be amenable to that proposition."

The words are hardly out of my mouth before Theo is striding down the hall, still holding me. I pay no attention to the layout of his house, too busy kissing my way across his scruff, until he pushes open a door with his foot. Beams of sunlight stream across the giant bed, illuminating the neatly made navy and white striped covers and Max, happily chewing on a bone in the corner.

"Max. Out."

Theo sets me down on the edge of his bed before crossing the room to close the door behind Max. Turning to me, he stalks back, unbuttoning his jeans as he approaches. I'm half tempted to scoot back, the intensity in his eyes ratcheting up both my nerves and my need for him.

Before I can protest, he's kneeling at the foot of the bed, wrapping his arms around my thighs and yanking me to the edge. "You are so beautiful." He kisses along my knee and up my inner thigh. His warm hands slide up the outside of my legs, toward my hips. He curls his fingers over the edge of my boy-short underwear and looks up at me, a question in his eyes. "May I?"

I lean back on my hands so I can lift my hips. "Please." He slides them down my legs and tosses them somewhere in the room. The way he trails his lips along my inner thigh, higher and higher, has my own need climbing with it.

Pulling my dress over my head, I toss it to the floor with the rest of our discarded clothes, leaving me in just my bra. Before he reaches my aching center, he slides along my body, his hands leading the way up my torso, followed by the rest of him.

"I can't decide which of your lips I need to taste more," he murmurs, settling on kissing my mouth as he guides my arms around his neck.

I whisper against his lips. "Just touch me—I don't care where." I'm so starved for touch, the lightest brush against my skin has me ready to detonate.

Theo stops, frowning down at me. "What do you mean? Tell me what you want, Sunshine."

Embarrassment at how dull my life has been floods through me, turning my skin splotchy red instead of a sexy blush. "I just...never mind. It doesn't matter. Just touch me." I pull Theo back down for a kiss, hoping to end the conversation.

"Sophie." The undertone of my name sends a shiver up my spine. It's a voice that expects to be obeyed. His fingers trace a path along my side, sending a flood of awareness through me. I close my eyes and focus on the way he's touching me, arching my back when he reaches under me to unhook my bra and slide it off. "Sophie, tell me what you meant." His voice is a whisper, his breath a caress along the sensitive skin of my breasts.

I sigh, not wanting to explain. "It's been so long since anyone has touched me. I can't pick because I want you to touch me everywhere."

He stills and worry that I've said something wrong fills me. Just when I'm sure he's going to tell me to leave, Theo lifts his face to look into mine.

Instead of judgment, I see lust, determination and even a hint of humor. "I love a challenge." He dips down to kiss me once more. "I have questions, but I don't want to think about anyone else right now. Close your eyes."

I do as he says, even though I want to keep them open and admire the muscles of his shoulders and the way his abs ripple as he moves.

"Am I allowed to touch you?" I whisper. It's the middle of the day, lawnmowers are running outside, cars are driving down the street, and I'm lying naked in my boss's bed as he runs his hands over every inch of my skin. It's so decadent I'm almost ashamed of myself.

There's a chuckle near my ear. "Sunshine, I've been dying for you to touch me since the night of the gala. Yes. Dear God, yes. Please touch."

I peek out from under my lashes before placing a hand on his chest. What starts as a tentative, slow exploration of each other turns desperate after my palm brushes over the bulge in the front of his jeans. Theo groans and responds by sliding a finger along my wet seam. "Can I taste you? Please?" His words send a bolt of lust straight through me.

My answering nod must be enough because immediately Theo pushes me up towards the head of the bed, while sliding himself down. There's no hesitation between the moment I stop moving and the second his tongue slides long and slow along me, then swirling around my clit. Fireworks explode behind my eyes and I cry out as an orgasm bursts through me. I've been dancing on the edge of wanting this man for weeks, thinking about him touching me, dreaming about the way he kissed me at the fundraiser. The climax that just rocketed through me was weeks in the making, floating at the edge of my mind at all hours of the day and night. "Oh, God." I moan.

"Has it been that long or should I be really pleased with myself right now?" The amused words floating up from the other end of the bed are accompanied by a finger sliding inside me. "You realize I'm not done with you yet, right?"

I don't have a chance to answer before he's at me again, his tongue flicking at my sensitive bundle of nerves, one finger, then two, pumping in and out. All of it combines to drive me back to the edge of another orgasm, but I breathe deep, holding it at bay for a moment while I enjoy the sensation of Theo spinning me higher.

My fingers slide through his hair, holding his head where I want it, even as my own thrashes from side to side on the pillow. "Theo, I need you. I need you inside me. Now." I manage to get out between moans.

"Can you reach the drawer on your left?" Theo pushes his jeans down off his hips. Wrapping his long fingers around his cock, he jerks his chin towards the drawer as he strokes himself. I'm so mesmerized by the girth of him, for a moment I forget what I'm doing. "Sunshine? Can you grab a condom?"

"What? Oh! Yes." I come back to Earth and reach into the drawer for a foil packet. "Sorry I forgot..." I trail off as I take in the sight in front of me—a literal Adonis kneeling on the bed, his lips stretched in a feral smile and his chin glistening with my own release.

Theo slides the condom on before stretching out on his side next to me, a hand on my hip to roll me towards him. "I want to see you, Sunshine." His voice is husky with need as he pulls me on top of his body.

I straddle his hips and take his thick cock in my hand, squeezing as I run my palm along its length a few times. "Keep that up and we'll be done much sooner than I planned." He grabs my hips, lifting me easily. I line him up with my entrance and ease myself down, eyes closed, concentrating on nothing but the sensation of him inside me. The fullness, the relief of finally having him fill me.

A deep groan echoes through the room. "You feel amazing, Sophie." Theo wraps his arms around my back, pulling me close for a kiss. I oblige before sitting back up, my hands braced against his perfect chest as I lift and lower myself.

What starts off as a slow, almost lazy pace, builds up speed until I can't keep up, my thighs burning with delicious heat. Theo grabs my hips and pumps into me from below while I clutch and claw at his chest. "Come for me," he commands and I know another orgasm is hovering, just out of reach. "I'm...so close. Tell me you're almost there, Sunshine. Please." Each word punctuated by the slamming of his hips into me.

"Almost...there," I gasp out. The breath is knocked out of me when Theo flips me onto my back, never losing our connection. He thrusts into me, faster and deeper. I don't hold back the cry that escapes me at this new sensation. His cock fills me, setting fire to all my nerve endings with each forceful movement.

"Fuck me. Sunshine, I need you to come." Sweat glistens on his forehead and our breath is ragged.

My orgasm builds in my chest, in my spine, in every cell of my body. Oxygen catches in my lungs and I soar to an unbearable high, climbing higher and higher without a way to come back down. Theo reaches between us and slides his thumb over my clit, sending me exploding over the edge and free-falling into my climax just as he groans and his own orgasm hits him. He swells inside me, triggering another satisfying little ripple through me. Not a full orgasm, but the sated waves of a spent body.

I try to wriggle out from under him, but don't get far before his arms are wrapped tight around me. "You promised not to run away."

"I wasn't running away." I laugh, but snuggle deeper into his arms. I don't know how long this is going to last—an hour, an afternoon, a weekend—but I'm not going to cut it short when I have nowhere else to be, or anyone to take care of. For once.

"Stay here." Theo kisses the shell of my ear before sliding off the bed. He comes back a moment later, condom disposed of, and a warm washcloth in hand. I take it and disappear into the adjoining bathroom before he can say a word. I pee and clean myself up before stepping back out. Theo is sitting on the edge of the bed, a corner of the covers pulled back, but his hands tucked between his knees.

He looks up as I exit and gives me a small smile. "I don't suppose I can convince you to stay here for the rest of the weekend, can I?"

"What?" He wants me to stay that long? Maybe so he can fully satisfy his curiosity about me before moving on. "Um, you want me to stay for the whole weekend? That was not...I wasn't...." I trail off at the hurt that creeps across his face.

"No pressure, Sunshine." He smiles at me, but it's a fake smile that doesn't reach his eyes.

If Lauren were here she would smack me upside the head for even considering leaving. My lady bits are voting with Lauren, probably so they can get another turn to play. I don't have a good excuse *not* to stay.

"Do you have a spare toothbrush?"

Fifteen

THEO

EARLY MORNING SUN SHINES in my eyes as I pull my game face
on. It's just another Monday at the office. I push the thought of
my amazing weekend with Sophie to the back of my mind where it
belongs so I can focus on my company. I grip my steering wheel, eyes
closed, head pressed hard into the back of my seat. After ten years of
doing this every day it should be second nature, but it's not. Every
morning, I put on my grumpy boss persona, just like my designer
suit coat. My armor.

I pull my phone out of my pocket and hold it up to my ear, the
podcast I had been listening to in the car still playing, the volume
turned low. Most days I really am on a phone call as I walk in, but
today I'm not above pretending, to avoid an awkward encounter
with Sophie.

I pull my eyebrows together, making my expression match the
tone of my voice. I keep up the charade, listening to the recording
as I pull my briefcase and coat out of the backseat.

"Unacceptable," I bark into the phone as I close the car door. One
of the ladies in marketing scurries past me.

"Yes, but don't you think that a book about a giant white whale should..." The podcast hosts mutter in my ear as I step inside.

"That's not what we agreed to. Check your contract—I think you'll find I'm correct." I cover my near-miss with a steely tone, furrowing my eyebrows for good measure.

"You don't think Ahab is just a lonely old man who's trying to go on one last..."

"Good morning, sir." Someone greets me, but I ignore them, my eyes straining to see through the windows into the lobby.

For all my famed smarts, I have no idea where things stand with Sophie. We spent the weekend wrapped up in each other in bed, ignoring reality. I haven't even asked her if she wants to see me again now the weekend is over. Because I may be a genius, but I'm also an idiot.

"I mean it, I have to go now." Sophie's laughing words from yesterday echo in my mind as I make my way to the front doors. My mouth twitches at the memory of her lips when I pulled her back for one more kiss. I'd convinced her to stay with me until it was time for her to pick up Emma. "Have a good night. And thank you for an amazing weekend—I'll never forget it."

Of course I spent all night dissecting what she'd meant. Was that a dismissal? Was Sophie done with me? Thirty-six hours is nowhere near long enough to unearth her secrets.

I slip my earbuds in, just in case my phone actually does ring, and pull open the door to the lobby. Sophie is bustling around her desk, doing whatever it is she needs to do to prepare for the day. I came in early hoping to see her without an audience. "Good morning." The greeting feels foreign on my tongue, probably because I never greet people unless they are coming to see me in my office.

Sophie keeps her eyes on her desk for a second before those blue depths look up at me. "Good morning Mr. Sutton." At my raised eyebrow she blushes, glancing around the lobby to make sure we're alone. "I don't...Am I supposed to pretend I don't know you? We never talked about..." She looks around again, fingers twisted together. No one else is here.

"I have no idea, Sunshine. I'm as lost as you." Before I can say anything else, Julian appears from the stairwell, a mug of coffee in each hand.

"Sir. Let me set this down and I'll call the elevator for you right away." He crosses the lobby to set a mug next to Sophie's elbow. "Here you go, Soph."

I have to suppress my urge to pull him away from my Sunshine. I want to be the one to bring her coffee, to call her by a nickname. She likes it with just a smidge of cream and sugar, which I learned yesterday morning when we surfaced from the bed long enough to refuel.

"Thank you Julian."

Do I dare say anything? I can't without giving away how I feel, so I content myself with drinking her in. The green and white polka dot dress she's wearing nips in at her waist, a white cardigan hangs over the back of her chair. Her blonde hair is curled and lays over her shoulders, catching in the morning sunlight. She looks happy and beautiful, the same as always. Maybe a smidge more relaxed than normal. I'm the one who's a nervous mess at the sight of her.

Instead of pulling her to me for a kiss, I walk over to the elevator banks and wait for the doors to open. I need a plan.

"Is there anything else you need, sir?" Mercedes pushes to her feet after going over the week's schedule with me.

"No, that will be all." I pause. "Actually, I do have one more thing. I believe I will have a guest coming with me to the Seattle event on Friday night. Can you make the arrangements?"

"Of course, sir." With that she leaves me to stare uselessly at my computer screen. I have emails to answer, meetings to prepare for, and code to write, but my mind is on one thing.

Me: Are you free Friday night? I have an event to go to and I'd enjoy your company.

I stare at my phone, willing her to answer, but all I get is silence. Finally, after five minutes of waiting, I push it aside and get to work. I can't even be mad, since Sophie's lack of answer proves she's not looking at her personal phone during office hours.

I manage to stay distracted until lunchtime. But when Mercedes sends me a message to let me know that she's leaving for her lunch break and that my lunch will be delivered in five minutes, the temptation is more than I can bear. Normally, when a delivery comes for me and Mercedes isn't here to pick it up, I wouldn't even notice who was responsible for walking it up to my office. But not today.

"This is Sophie, how can I help you?" Her voice is enough to make my dick twitch in my slacks.

"Sunshine." I growl out.

"Yes sir, what can I do for you?" Is she teasing me? I swear, I can hear it in her tone.

"Mercedes ordered lunch for me. Will you bring it up to my office when it arrives?"

There's a long pause. "I was just about to step away from the desk for my lunch break. I'll have Tina bring it up when it arrives."

Sophie hangs up the phone before I can speak, leaving me fuming. I'm a jumble of indignation that she doesn't want to see me, and insecurity that I've done something to upset her.

Me: I need to talk to you, Sunshine.

There's a timid knock on my office door ten minutes later. Pushing back from my giant desk, I cross my office to open the door. The other girl from the front desk, not-Sophie, is standing on the other side, a brown paper bag in her hand. Her eyes go wide at the sight of me.

"What do you want?" I snap.

"H-here you go Mr. Sutton. There's silverware in the bag." She shoves the bag at me, whirling away when I take it and hurrying to the elevator doors. Annoyed that I won't get to see Sophie again, I slam the door a little harder than necessary and take the bag to my desk. No longer hungry, I leave it and go back to the never-ending list of emails and crises vying for my attention.

I'm in the middle of typing out a curt response to yet another request for an interview for yet another tech-startup magazine, when there's another knock on my door.

"What now?" I growl out as I fling the door open.

A narrow-eyed Sophie is waiting for me on the other side. "Hello to you, too. I just came to tell you I can't go with you on Friday night."

She turns away before I can react, but I snag the back of her elbow to stop her and pull her into my office, shutting the door behind us.

"I'm sorry." I lean in close, letting the scent of her drift through me. "I didn't mean to growl at you."

Sophie cocks a hip, her arms crossed over her delicious chest. "You mean, you didn't intend to yell at *me*. But yelling at Tina is okay?" She shakes her head. "Do your grumpy boss thing—you're the CEO, right? I can't go with you on Friday. That's all I came to say."

Instead of grabbing her by the hips and bending her over my desk like I want to, I content myself with rubbing my hands over her upper arms. "I'll try not to frighten the staff in the future. Why can't you come? Do you not want to see me again?"

Sophie slumps, leaning into my touch. "I just...we're just..." She waves a hand around my office and takes a visible breath. "Listen, Mr. Sutton. The weekend was amazing. Thank you for making me feel, well, feel like something other than a sad, lonely, single-mom for a moment. I will treasure that memory for a long time. But we both know there's no way this can work out."

I recoil at her words. This is not what I want to hear, not the kind of speech I was hoping for from her. What did I expect? That she'd fall at my feet at the offer? Isn't that exactly what I don't want? The reason I like her is that she *doesn't* treat me like I can do no wrong.

What if she only came over because I'm her boss and she was scared of the consequences? Have I become *that guy*?

"Sunshine. Sophie. Did you, um, did you not enjoy yourself this weekend?" I force myself to ask the question. Why else would she be saying no? I don't step away, but I can't look at her, can't bear to see the pity in her eyes when she tells me her excuse.

A soft hand against my cheek has me turning back to look at her. "Theo," Sophie whispers, her eyes sincere. "The weekend was amazing. Truly. I'm sore in places I forgot could be sore." Her cheeks go pink. "But, well, you're *you* and I'm just me. Let's leave it at that, okay? A wonderful memory, untouched by reality."

This time she does walk away, and I let her, ignoring the snick of my office door closing as I slump down on the couch. I never even had a chance to tell her that I was going to take her to Seattle for the night. I've never wanted to prove to a woman that I have more money than I can spend before, but Sophie? I'd spend every penny on her if she'd let me.

Well, if she won't come when I ask nicely, maybe *I* won't ask.

Being the boss has to be good for something, right?

Sixteen

SOPHIE

DEAR MS. PRICE,

Your attendance is required at the 4th Annual Tech for Teens fundraising gala this Friday at 8pm. As this is a work-sponsored trip, Mailbox will arrange for your transportation to and from the event. Your transport will meet you at Mailbox at 7pm, sharp. Black-tie dress. Please acquire the appropriate attire and submit your receipts for reimbursement.

I wave my phone under Lauren's nose as she follows me into my house. "What is this? Did you do this?"

Laughing, Lauren grabs the phone, her amusement audibly dropping as she reads the email. "What? No. I didn't have anything to do with it. That's from Sutton's Executive Assistant. He must have asked her to send it to you directly."

I busy myself looking through the bottles of three-buck Chuck in the cupboard, avoiding eye contact. If Lauren sees my face, I'll give something away.

"Sophie? What happened? I thought you said your gala evening with Sutton was a disaster? Why would he invite you again unless...Soph. You didn't! Tell me nothing else happened." She grins. "Better yet, tell me something *did*."

I continue avoiding eye contact, searching for my electric bottle opener. A hand holds it in front of my face a second later. When I don't move to take it, Lauren takes the bottle clutched in my hand and pulls the foil cap off. "Spill."

"Well. See. I mayhavekissedSuttoninthelimo." The words come out all in one breath.

"You...kissed Theodore-sexiest-man-alive Sutton and you *didn't tell me?*" Lauren's screech is echoed from Emma's room.

"Mom!" Her head pokes out of the bedroom. "You did what?" Emma comes bounding out, already in her pajamas. Or has she been in them all day? She was silent and broody in the car on the way home last night and still asleep when I left for work this morning. "Wait, is that why you and Teddy were all weird when we found his dog?"

Lauren pours the wine, splashing a bit on the counter at Emma's words. "Wait. Hang on. Why am I the last to know? You found his dog?" Lauren eyes my kid. "Teddy? Did you just call the scariest, grumpiest man on the face of the Earth, *Teddy*? The man is a bear all right—the kind that'll rip your head off just for fun." She stops asking questions just long enough to take a sip of her wine. "Talk. Now, missy."

I'm not getting out of this. If these two gang up on me, I'll never have a moment of peace. "There was some kissing in the limo after the gala."

"Go, Mom!"

At my glare, Emma mimes zipping her lips before gesturing for me to continue.

"I know there's more. What about the dog-finding?" Lauren's question has Emma's ears turning pink.

"Um, that was kind of my fault." Emma squeaks. "I had Max outside on Friday after you dropped him off, Aunt Lauren. There was this SUV of dude bros and I maaaaay have flipped them off when they cat-called me. They honked and Max got away from me. I was looking for him when Teddy came around the corner looking for his dog. Did you know his dog is also named Max?"

"Okay, first of all, high-five for flipping them off, way to smash the patriarchy. Second, if I check your TikTok will there be another video of Max? Cause you know I live for that shit. Should we make him his own account?" Lauren stops to take a sip of wine. "Never mind, not the important thing. Teddy? How the fuck are you on a first name basis with Mr. Sutton? And what happened with the lost dog and cat situation?"

"Lauren, can you *try* to keep it to one curse word per speech? I like to pretend I'm a good mom." I can't help the heavy sigh that escapes me at her words.

"Mom." Emma rolls her eyes. "You stopped caring if I swore at home when we had to struggle through Algebra together."

We all raise a fist in the air and yell "Fuck algebra!" then resume the conversation without missing a beat.

"It's math. The rules are different." I raise an eyebrow at Emma over the edge of my wine glass. "Continue."

Sticking her tongue out at me for a second, Emma finishes her side of the story. "Anyways, Teddy found Max, our Max, and sent me a text to let me know. We hopped in the car to go pick him up and I saw his Max nosing around someone's yard on the way. So we traded his Max for our Max before Mom took me over to Dad's house for the weekend. Which *sucked* by the way, not that anyone cares what I think about it."

"And your mom was weird with Mr. Sutton? Was he weird with her?" Lauren asks, ignoring me.

"Duh. Mom is always weird. But he was kind of flirty? But also not? I dunno." Emma shrugs. "I kind of forgot it all since my weekend was terrible and *no one cares*."

Irritated at her dramatics, I take a long sip of wine before responding. "Sweetie, you know I have to stick to the custody arrangement. I'm sorry it was boring."

"It wasn't boring, Mom. He spent the whole weekend hanging out with his girlfriend." Her eyes open wide at the confession.

My body goes still. Slowly, I set my wine glass down before I break it. "You didn't say anything about his girlfriend. Did she go with you to your doctor's appointment?" Anger builds in my gut, mixed with a healthy dose of guilt. I'd been off playing sexy weekend with Theo, while Emma was forced to play happy family with the woman her father had been cheating on me with. I count to ten in my head so I don't lose my shit at Emma instead of Jake.

Lauren asks my question before I can get past five. "Hang on. Why didn't you say anything about this before?"

Guilt flashes across Emma's face, her shoulders hunching forward. "I didn't want to upset you. We....uh...didn't go to my appointment." Her voice gets smaller and smaller as she speaks, until the last word is barely a whisper.

"What the ever-loving FUCK is wrong with that man?" Lauren yells for me.

All the missed events of our past come flooding back to me. Dentist appointments, school assemblies, play-dates—how many times had he missed one because he was too busy with his own hobbies? The guilt and anger in my gut boil over into a white-hot rage.

I don't yell. I don't shout. I pull out my phone and dial, holding up a finger as I lift it to my ear.

It goes to voicemail.

"You want to tell me why you couldn't be bothered to take your daughter to her annual check-up? What. The. Fuck. Is. Wrong. With. You?" I grind the words out between my teeth. "Are you so busy doting on your shiny new toy that you can't be bothered to make sure your actual daughter is healthy? Did your child-bride have her own doctor's appointment to go to?"

Emma's mouth drops open and her eyes go wide at my words. I should have known.

"I can tell from the look on your daughter's face that I guessed correctly. Listen very carefully to me Jake—if you ever pull this kind of shit again I will not only make sure you lose all custody of Emma, but I will take you to court for every fucking penny you don't have. Explain *that* to your new baby-mama." I'm about to hang up, overflowing with righteous anger when another thought occurs to me. "You owe Emma an apology. I'll be checking that it happens." I hang up, dropping my phone on the kitchen counter.

"Daaaaamn, Soph. That was hot." Lauren's shocked look is replaced by a grin as she nudges my wine glass towards me. "Okay, so to sum up the weekend. You had a moment with Sutton, Emma got shafted by Jake, and now Sutton wants you to go to some event on Friday night? I feel like I'm missing something here. Does he know Elinor Price is your pen name?"

"Emma, I love you sweetie. I'm sorry your dad was an ass this weekend." I pull her in for a hug and kiss the top of her head. "But go away for a second."

"I always miss the good stuff." Emma whines, but I don't budge, just wait for her to walk away. "Fine. You have five minutes. I have to pee anyway." She stomps the fifteen feet to her door and flips it closed.

"Theo asked me to meet him for coffee on Saturday morning. And I may have slept over that night." If I thought saying it fast would somehow lessen the impact of my words I was sorely mistaken.

"You...slept with him?" Lauren's eyes are open wide enough to rival the anime characters Emma loves. "You. Sophie Alexander, who's never slept with anyone aside from Jake, had s-e-x with our boss?"

I wait for her to judge, to tell me what a bad idea it is, to help me come to my senses. Lauren puts her wine glass down on the counter with care before stepping close.

"I'm so fucking proud of you!" Her arms are wrapping me up in a bear hug before her words register. "My baby girl is finally doing something for herself."

"Wait, you're not shocked? You don't think it's the stupidest thing I've ever done?" I'm the one in shock now. I was sure Lauren was going to talk sense into me. Someone needs to. "You're not going to tell me to stay away from him? I was counting on you telling me not to go to this event on Friday."

Lauren lets go and eyes me. "Oh my God, you want to go, don't you?"

I can't hide my indecision from my best friend. "First things first, everything was consensual, right? He didn't pressure you or threaten your job did he?"

I shake my head. "No, he didn't. It was, uh, definitely consensual." My cheeks flame at the memory.

"So, then the next question, was the sex good? Your blush tells me it was." Lauren grins at me, picking up her wine glass for another sip. The toilet flushing in the bathroom warns me we've only got another minute to discuss the situation.

"Yes, it was good. Yes, I would do it again if the opportunity presented itself."

Lauren sways her hips from side to side in a celebratory dance. "Oh yeah, we gotta make that happen. I don't know if I understand the attraction—he seems like a real grouch to me—but if anyone has earned some fun and great orgasms it's you."

We clink our wine glasses together as Emma emerges from the room. Lauren winks at me before pulling Emma against her side.

"Emma, you and I are having a sleepover on Friday night. Should we dye our hair or get matching tattoos?"

"No tattoos." I struggle to suppress my grin at the mischievous look on both their faces.

"You're such a party-pooper, Mom. Ugh. I guess it wouldn't be fun if you didn't get the matching tattoo with us. We'll just get matching piercings instead. I was thinking a nose ring, maybe?"

Laughing, she and Lauren start comparing the pros and cons of various piercings while I wander over to sit on the couch.

I don't know what to think of Theo's invitation. He addressed it to Elinor—does that mean it's purely a work-related event? Is he trying to hide that he's dating an employee? Is he embarrassed to be seen dating the receptionist? Or is he trying to shield me from the questions that would inevitably come my way if word got out?

I want to believe the best of him, that he's attempting to protect me. But the reality is that men like him—handsome, rich, connected—don't date nobodies like me. Not without consequences.

And he won't be the one facing them.

I'm torn between my desire to forget everything and spend the evening with Theo, and the responsible part of my brain that's screaming to end it now before things get complicated.

But I want to see him, enjoy his company. The same way we enjoyed each other's company at the fundraiser and at the dog park. His dry wit, the glimpses of thoughtfulness and compassion that he keeps carefully hidden from the world, his intelligence—they all turn me on more than I want to admit.

Emma flops on the couch next to me, laying her head in my lap. "Mom, you should go." Lauren sprawls on the other side of me, hooking one leg underneath her so she can face me. The three of us have spent many nights either on my couch or on Lauren's, in this exact configuration. Me in the middle, my two girls on either side.

Lauren pokes my cheek. "I can hear you overthinking. Just go. Emma and I will have a girl's night, probably torture Max into hiding under the bed, and you get a chance to do something new."

"Maybe I wanted to be part of the girl's night?" I poke Emma's forehead.

"Sophie Marie Alexander, you are going. You're going to go and you're going to feel beautiful and wanted and appreciated. It doesn't matter if this is the only time you ever go out with Theodore again, but you are going to have this night. Even if I have to kidnap and toss you in his Audi myself."

"You know what this means, right?" Emma says, peering up at Lauren from my lap. "We get to go shopping again!"

Seventeen

THEO

"HI CASEY."

Ethan and Clara are making a racket in the background, banging what sounds like an entire kitchen's worth of pots and pans.

"Hey, Teddy. How's it going?"

"I feel like I should send reinforcements. How are they this loud so early in the morning?"

My sister's exasperated sigh echoes in my head from my earbuds. "Don't start with me—they've been up for hours. But if reinforcements means you're coming to visit soon, I would absolutely love some. Garrett's only been gone a week and I'm already about to lose my mind." A loud crash reaches me through the phone. "Ethan! Do not climb on the counter. Hang on."

Her footsteps and hushed telling off are drowned out by a new voice on the line. "Ha? Hi hi."

"Hi hi, baby." Clara makes strange almost-words in my ear. "It's Uncle Teddy. Can you say Uncle Teddy?" She doesn't, but the babbling in my ear is adorable, pulling a smile from me as I open the door.

I'm a dozen steps inside before I realize that there are two, no three, people staring at me as if I've lost my mind. And one person smiling at me like she's found a treasure.

My Sunshine.

Also, shit. I pull my lips down into a scowl, glaring at Julian and Ms. Masterson. "Uncle Teddy? When are you coming to visit?" Ethan asks, startling me.

"I'm not sure buddy. Soon."

Casey calls his name in the background and the sound of the phone being dropped explodes in my ear.

"Sorry, Teddy. Call you later?" Casey says in my ear.

"Sure."

She says a hurried goodbye and hangs up as I get to the reception desk.

Tina, that's her name, scurries away as soon as I make eye-contact, while Julian jogs over to the elevator bank. I hold up a finger for him to wait, stopping at Sophie's desk. Ms. Masterson doesn't speak, just slides over from her perch on the edge of the desk to make room for me. I glare at her but she just gives me a blank look back.

"Ms. Price asked me to pass on a message to you, sir." Sophie's voice wavers for a moment before she clears her throat.

"Yes?"

"She wanted me to let you know she received your email regarding this weekend and that she is looking forward to it."

A face-splitting grin escapes me before I can school it back into my usual scowl and I tap the desk. "Excellent. I'll be in touch with her to make arrangements."

I don't trust myself not to do something stupid like pull her into my arms and kiss her soundly, so I walk away, not looking back. But as the elevator doors start to close, I'm sure I hear Tina's voice. "Was he...smiling?"

By Friday, the struggle to keep up my morning routine is painful. I've been coming into the office earlier and earlier to avoid passing Sunshine's desk with an audience. Today, I beat her to the office, but by ten in the morning I'm in desperate need of her smile so I wander downstairs and out to my car for no reason other than to get a glimpse of her.

Of course, she's much better at acting professionally than I am and continues her phone conversation as I walk past the first time, giving me nothing more than a head nod. The second time I pass her, a hint of a smile graces those luscious lips, but it isn't enough. I need the real thing. So I spin on my heel, make some kind of exasperated noise and go back to my car. After the shocked look on her face as I pass her a third time, she finishes her phone call, giving me the opportunity to stop and speak to her.

"Good morning, Ms. Alexander."

"Good morning, Mr. Sutton. Is there something I can do for you today?"

I pause, aware that Tina is listening to our conversation. "No thank you. I just wanted to double check that Ms. Price's phone had been returned to her."

Sophie bites her lips, is she trying not to laugh at me? I pull my eyebrows together and glare. "Yes sir, she has it." A subtle movement of her left hand draws my eye, revealing her phone tucked to the side of her keyboard.

I nod. "Good, good. I wouldn't want her to miss any important messages." Needing to abort before I say anything else stupid, I head to the elevator without another word. My phone buzzes in my pocket as the door opens on the top floor.

Sunshine: *Did you actually need something from your car? Or was that badly acted performance for my sake?*

Grinning, I type out a response.

Me: Badly acted? I would be offended, Sunshine, but my sister most assuredly inherited all the acting skill in our family. Although, I believe that my niece Clara may end up giving her a run for her money.

We text sporadically throughout the day, revealing tantalizing tidbits about ourselves.

Sunshine: Are you allergic to anything?

Me: No. Are you?

Sunshine: Vicodin—no foods though. I don't particularly like shellfish, something about the texture just doesn't do it for me. Sometimes I say I'm allergic, to get out of eating it.

Me: So flying you to Maine for fresh lobster wouldn't be your idea of a good date? Noted.

It takes her entirely too long to answer, but again, I can't be mad, knowing she's doing her job and doing it well. Damn her excellent work ethic.

Sunshine: Flying me anywhere for a date is unnecessary.

Me: *Challenge accepted.*

Her text has me amending my plan for tonight. It will take longer to get there, but it will be worth it.

I don't bother going home, choosing instead to change at the office. Mercedes leaves me at her usual five-thirty, hiding a smile at my change in plans.

"Goodnight, sir. I hope Ms. Price appreciates the date you've cooked up for her."

"Have a good weekend, Mercedes," I call back to her. "It's an event, not a date."

"If you say so. You know, I wash my grandbabies' mouths out with soap when they lie to me."

A month ago, I would have growled out a response, stuck my head out, and made some kind of vague threat, but knowing I'm going to see my Sunshine any minute, has me smiling instead.

"Mercedes…"

She sticks her head through my office door, eyebrow raised. I point at her. "If my 'scary boss' reputation is ruined, I'll know exactly who to blame."

She just smiles at me like I was one of her grandbabies. "You mean yourself? If you want to keep up 'your reputation', as you put it, you'll have to stop walking around here with a smile on your face and making excuses to talk to Ms. Alexander as you go through the lobby. Have fun!" She left before I could snap out an argument.

The muted ding of the elevator doors opening twenty minutes later pulls me from the project I'd been going over.

"Hello?" Sophie's soft voice drifted through my doorway.

I come out to meet her, pulling my tuxedo jacket on and buttoning it, stopping short at the sight of her. "Wow. You look…" I can't find words to describe how beautiful she is.

The emerald green dress she's wearing has wide bands of fabric that crisscross over her chest, sitting off the edge of her shoulders, before wrapping around her narrow waist and flaring out into a full skirt. Her usual June Cleaver look has been bumped up to Marilyn Monroe, the low dip in the front of the dress barely containing her generous breasts and her smooth calves peeking out from under the knee-length skirt. Her curled hair drifts over her collar bones, teasing me with glimpses of her bare shoulders.

"Is it okay?" The worry in her tone and the way she's working her bottom lip with her teeth has me across the space in a few long strides.

Pinching her chin with one hand, the other wrapping around her waist, I pull her plump bottom lip free. "You're breathtaking." I murmur the words against her lips, brushing hers with mine. "Damn, I want to rip this dress off you and kiss all the lipstick off your face."

"Don't you dare!" Sophie laughs, pushing me away. "You are not ripping off a dress that cost more than my monthly grocery budget, especially one with such fabulous pockets." She demonstrates by shoving her hands deep into the sides of her dress. "And Emma will kill me if you mess up my hair or makeup."

"I'll buy you a new dress. I'll buy you all the dresses you could ever want, if you promise me I can rip them off you later." There's a hint of teasing to my words, but the moment they leave me I want to take them back.

The light in Sophie's eyes dims just a fraction and she steps back, putting more distance between us. "So, where is this event? I know it's not in the building, I would know if you were throwing a black tie event in one of the conference rooms." Something's wrong, her words are forced, her enthusiasm fake.

Pushing aside the weird tension between us, I hold out my arm to her. "Well, you told me I wasn't allowed to fly you to Maine for a date."

"I said you aren't allowed to fly me *anywhere* for just a date."

I pull her to the elevator and push the button to take us to the roof. Instead of answering her question, I tug her into my arms and spend a moment in silence feeling her curves against me. "Theo?"

Her voice is husky and ends with a shiver as I trace my fingers across the exposed skin of her back and arms.

"Just wait," I whisper against her neck, dipping my head to kiss her temple. If I kiss her lips or her neck, I won't stop. Instead I close my eyes and let the smell of her perfume—citrus and sunshine—drift into my soul.

The elevator stops and the doors open with a whoosh, the deafening whir of my surprise drowning out all the other noises of the summer night.

"A helicopter?" Sophie shouts in my ear.

Pulling back, I grin. "It's not a plane." Before she can come up with any objections, I lead her across the roof and help her climb inside. We settle in, slip the protective headsets over our ears, and buckle in.

"Where are you taking me? Not Maine, I hope!" Sophie's words crackle through the headset, her grin back in place.

"No, not Maine. Just Seattle."

"*Just* Seattle, he says. Like a helicopter ride from Portland to Seattle is just a normal, ordinary thing to do on a Friday night." I can't tell if she's talking to herself or me.

"You know we can both hear everything you say, right?" I point to the pilot and myself.

It's still light out, making it easy to see the blush that creeps over her cheeks and chest. "Well, now I do."

Laughing, I tuck her under my arm, wanting to be close, and let the pilot do his thing. He points out interesting landmarks as we make the hour and a half flight, not that I'm paying much attention. Sophie soaks up every word, asking questions about things she spots and about the pilot himself. I'm too busy drinking her in—the warmth of her against my side, the sound of her laugh and gasps of surprise. The way her hair catches the light and how her skin glows, it captivates me.

We touch down on the hotel roof as the sun dips into the Pacific, the riot of shadow and light doing nothing to hide Sophie's expressions of delight. I help her climb out of the helicopter, when her heel catches on something and she almost falls out. I barely restrain myself from throwing her over my shoulder and carrying her to the door

"Thank you!" She calls with a giggle to our pilot. He gives her a friendly wave before climbing back in. "Oh!" She looks up at me with those big eyes. "Is he leaving? How are we getting home?"

"He's just going to the airfield nearby to make room for anyone else who needs the helipad." I tuck her hand into the crook of my elbow and lead her to the elevator. "As for when we're going home, that's up to you to decide. We can leave whenever you want. Tonight, or in the morning."

Stepping into the open doors, I pull Sophie in front of me, wrapping my arms around her waist, her hands settling over mine. If she can feel my already semi-hard cock pressing against her ass, she doesn't give me any clue, but she does tip her head to the side, exposing the long line of her throat. I trace my lips and tongue along it, as she leans against me.

"Mmmm. That feels so good." Her quiet words escape as I let my tongue slip out, tasting her.

"You're in charge."

She twists to look me in the eye. "Again? I could get used to this." The way her mouth twitches at her teasing words, and the twinkle in her eye, are proof I've said the words she needed to hear.

The elevator ride is over before I can follow up her teasing, the doors slide open to the ballroom and our reason for being here. It's easy to pick out the donors versus the teens and their families who were invited to come and show us what our money is doing. Presentation boards dot the edges of the rooms, like a science fair, and nervous, sweaty teens hover in front of them.

I don't go to most functions because I enjoy it. I go because I'm expected to and I support their causes—but this particular event is one I look forward to every year. "Come." I adjust Sophie's hand in my elbow and pull her to the edge of the room. "Let's go see the future of technology."

The nervous young lady we approach first gives us a wobbly explanation of her app, her voice so soft I have to strain to hear it. Sophie leans against me and smiles at her, encouraging the teen to continue. When the girl stammers again and I lean close, Sophie looks up at my face and frowns.

"Sorry hun, let me fix his face for you." Before I can figure out what she means, Sophie's fingers are pushing the corners of my mouth up in a grimace, then smoothing over my brow. "He's worked so hard to perfect the scowl, sometimes he doesn't know how to turn it off." Sophie laughs over her shoulder before thumping mine. An answering giggle from the teen is her reward. "Stop scaring the poor girl. She's not an employee you have to terrify."

I can't help my chuckle at her antics, the tension in my shoulders floating away with the sound of her laugh. The teenager starts her presentation over, much more relaxed, and tells us about how her app can calculate and track an individual's carbon footprint based off their consumer habits. There are some obvious flaws in the plan, like security and the self-selection of those who would choose to use it, but I file the idea away in my mind along with the girl's name. Maybe I'll be in touch after she graduates from college in a few years. I add to my mental note to look into what kind of scholarship she's been awarded by the organization, maybe I can boost it.

This is why this is my favorite event of the year. And having Sophie here, awed and asking questions of the kids, relaxing them into telling us more, is better than it's ever been. Sophie has a knack with the teens—she taps into their natural enthusiasm in a way I've never been able to. Maybe it's because of Emma, maybe it's because she's just that warm and beautiful inside.

We drift around the room, chatting to people as we go. Sophie's arm tucked inside my elbow fills me with a sense of rightness I've never felt before. I'm relaxed and chatting with whoever she stops to talk to and introducing her to the people I know in the room. Being based in Seattle, this non-profit attracts support from the high-powered tech industry nearby.

"Oh, that smells divine, what is it?" Sophie stops a server walking past us with a tray of little pastries. She has one in her mouth before the server has a chance to answer. The way her cheeks puff like a chipmunk as she chews is adorable, and the little moan she makes at the taste has my cock eager to join the party.

"It's an artichoke and feta tart, ma'am."

Sophie swallows her bite and holds the rest of it towards me. "They're delicious. Theo, you have to try this." Without thinking, I open my mouth and take the bite from her. My lips close over the tips of her fingers, and I can't help the way my tongue snakes out to give them a swipe as well. Sophie's eyes go wide at the action before mischief fills them. Instead of pulling her hand back, she lets her fingers linger, her thumb swiping at my bottom lip. Pinching my chin between her thumb and forefinger, she draws me close. I'm disappointed when she doesn't pull me in for a kiss, but instead brings her lips millimeters from my ear.

"I'm ready to leave, but I'm not ready to go home." She pulls back, eyes never leaving mine as her hand moves to caress my cheek. "I've heard this hotel makes the most delicious waffles for breakfast. Think I could try them?"

I slide my arm around her waist and pull her against me, not caring who else in the room sees. "I believe that can be arranged." I dip my head down to whisper in her ear. "I'll order you the entire room-service menu if it means I get to lick it off every inch of you."

An adorable blush reddens her cheeks and her hands come to rest on my forearms. She cocks her head to one side, the edge of her lip caught between her teeth. "Is that a promise?"

Grinning, I take her by the hand and pull her toward the exit, getting us upstairs to the room I had Mercedes book for me the only thing on my mind. Technically, she booked two rooms for tonight, one for me and one for Elinor Price, but I'll be damned if Sophie sleeps anywhere but in my bed. Not that I plan on sleeping.

Eighteen

THEO

"SHOULD I BOTHER ASKING how you already have a hotel room key? Or is that one of those things that magically happens when you have a lot of money?" Sophie's laugh dances over me, warming me from the inside as I unlock the door.

"It's called Mercedes is magical and I need to give her another raise." I push the door open and pull her in after me, stopping to flip a light on.

"Oh!" Sophie sneaks past me and makes a beeline for the huge picture window on one side of the suite. Instead of the typical view of downtown Seattle, our window looks out toward the Pacific. The inky blackness of the ocean stretches out below. "Mercedes is lovely. She always stops to chat with me on her way to lunch."

I pull my jacket off and drape it over a nearby chair, pulling one end of my bowtie free. "Sunshine," I growl, eyes locked on the dip of her waist, knowing her perfectly round ass is hiding beneath the full skirt of her dress.

She doesn't turn, but gives me a sly look over her shoulder, eyes going big as I stalk closer. "Y-yes?"

"My assistant is amazing, but I don't want to talk about her right now." I take the last few steps to her, undoing the top two buttons of my shirt. Not waiting for her to respond, my hands go to her sides as I step behind her, bringing us both against the cold glass.

Sophie presses her hands against the window, her body pushing back against mine—her head tilted, still looking back at me. I bend down to capture her lips, tasting the champagne she'd had earlier, but also something that was uniquely her. She tastes like everything I've been missing in my life.

With a groan, I turn her to face me so her back is against the window. My lips never leave hers as we kiss. Kiss is too small a word for what's happening between us. I devour her, she consumes me. Sophie's lips promise me heaven. A safe-haven from the world, a place where I can be everything and nothing, but always enough.

Like a broken Japanese dish, repaired with gold and made more beautiful by the evidence of a life well-lived, Sophie's kiss finds all the tiny cracks inside me, filling them with her warmth. I don't know how to do the same for her. I know she's just as broken inside as I am and has had her own share of disappointments and hardships. Different to mine, but equal in pain. For someone who's been called the smartest man in the room since I was a teenager, I'm lost when it comes to Sophie. All I know is that I will do whatever it takes to make her feel as safe as she makes me feel.

Exploring her curves with my hands, I slide them up her sides and along her arms, lifting them up above her before bracing my forearms on either side of her head. Cradling, caging, cocooning us in a world that consists of nothing but our bodies, hungry for each other. Her desperate fingers tug at the buttons of my shirt, fumbling and failing to get them undone.

"Why...are these...so goddamn tiny!" Her frustrated words are punctuated by harder and harder tugs at the fabric. My chuckle only seems to wind her up more and her hands move from the buttons to tugging the shirt out of my slacks, like she can't make up her mind what she wants, only that she wants it immediately.

"Do you need help?" I pull away from the line I've been kissing along her jaw as she grunts in annoyance.

"No. I can do it. They're fucking buttons."

"You could just rip them." I offer up, sliding my lips across one perfectly bared shoulder. "Or I could stop kissing you and help."

"Don't. You. Dare. No stopping. Keep kissing. Buttons will not defeat me." Her words are lost in the sensation of her hands sliding up my chest beneath the shirt, and her gasp as I bite down on her ear lobe.

"Belt. Belt is easier," she whispers. Her hands follow her words, tugging at the belt buckle until it comes undone. The hook and zipper of my slacks follow suit. "Thank fuck." Her hands plunge inside and she's got a firm grip on my ass before I can do more than groan at the invasion. "Zipper. Get the zipper on my dress." She whispers over and over before I delve back into kissing her.

Smiling against her lips, I step back, her grip on me dragging her away from the window. My wandering fingers found the zipper pull earlier tonight, flicking it inadvertently when I couldn't resist sliding a hand along her spine. I take my time now, cradling the back of her head with one hand, using it to deepen our kiss, while my free hand pulls the zipper with excruciating slowness. I pull back when I get the zipper all the way down and nothing happens.

"There's a hook at the top." Sophie says, freeing her hands and grinning at me. Lifting her hands, she brushes the side of my face, sliding her fingers into the hair at my temple. Spell-bound, I lean into her touch, another crack in my heart filling with her golden light, even as my fingers find the offending hook and flick it open.

The dress falls open, then drops to the ground as Sophie lowers her arms, leaving her standing in a pool of emerald fabric. I want to drop to my knees and worship her at the sight. My sweet, innocent Sunshine was hiding a sinful Aphrodite beneath that dress. She's a goddess, a temptress, her curves wrapped not in the bra and panties I was expecting, but in a peach lace corset, complete with garters holding up a pair of thigh-high stockings.

"Sunshine..." It's all I can get out before I'm on my knees in front of her. "Fuck me. I may have just swallowed my tongue." I run my hands over her torso, the lace and satin teasing my fingertips. My lips follow as my hands slide around her hips, grabbing her ass like she grabbed mine, pulling her sweet pussy towards my face. A desperate need to taste her fills me.

Her strained chuckle stops me. "I was hoping to escape the weekend without any emergencies." It's not her words, it's the tension in her body that has me looking up at her. "Is it...?" She swallows. "I wasn't sure if you'd like it."

"Like it?" I surge to my feet, cupping the back of her legs and picking her up in one go. "Sunshine, you're the sexiest fucking thing I've ever seen."

"But—"

"If you'd asked me an hour ago how I wanted to die, I would have said in my sleep, sixty years from now." I walk us to the bedroom, Sophie's legs wrapped around my hips, the heat of her pussy against my cock exquisite agony with each step.

"And now?"

"I'm pretty sure my heart stopped the second your dress hit the ground, because seeing you in that can only mean I'm in paradise."

I set her down, my eyes never leaving her face as she sits on the edge of the bed. I toe off my shoes and unbutton the shirt she was too flustered to manage earlier. She leans back on her hands, ankles crossed as she waits. I finish stripping out of my clothes, my cock standing at attention the second I free it.

"Fuck Sophie, I can't decide what I want to do first. Now I know how you felt last time. Do I feast on that sweet pussy? Or do I peel those stockings off you one at a time, preferably with my teeth? Do I have enough self-control not to flip you on your hands and knees and fuck you from behind? But the way your tits are spilling out the top of that..."

"Yes." It's dark in the room, but not so dark I can't see the way her eyes close as she sighs the word. As if just my words are enough to make her come.

"To what?"

Her eyes snap open and she stares me down, challenging me. "All of it. Starting with the stockings."

"Morning, Sunshine." Sophie's arm flaps wildly in my direction, missing my face by an inch. Chuckling, I continue kissing my way along the silky-smooth skin of her back, my fingers roaming over her stomach. Her answering groan could be from pleasure or because she wants to go back to sleep.

"It's too early, please don't make me get up." The pillow muffles her grumble. She's curled up on her side in the middle of the bed, the covers gathered up in her arms in front of her, hands adorably tucked up under her chin. "I'm enjoying this glorious bed."

"You don't have to wake up, just lay there." I'd woken up earlier with her back pressed up against my chest, her head tucked under my chin. I'd contented myself with spooning for a while, even if that delicious ass nestled up against my dick was torture. But the need to touch her, to make sure this was real, won out.

My hand on her stomach draws circles, a little wider each time, until I'm grazing the underside of her breasts and the patch of curly hair between her legs. I smile at her tiny whimper when I kiss along the back of her neck. Teasing the full swell of her breasts, my lips make their way to her exposed neck. I shift my hips, pressing my erection against her, so I can reach the spot behind her ear. I could spend all day exploring every inch of Sophie's body.

Groaning, her body goes limp, her thighs relaxing against mine, as I suck her earlobe between my lips. I slide my hand down her soft stomach and that's all it takes to roll her onto her back, body limp and pliable.

"You're mean." Her small smile takes the sting out of her words and I can't help my smirk, even though she can't see it with her eyes still closed. "You tease a girl with a good night's sleep in this big, glorious bed, and then you keep waking her up for amazing sex. You really are the worst."

"If you want me to stop, just say the word." I leave a trail of kisses starting from the back of her ear, down her neck and between those glorious tits.

Sophie's body shifts beneath me, stiffening as she does a full-body stretch accompanied by a cartoonish yawn. "Don't you dare stop." Her hands come to rest on the back of my head as her body relaxes back into the mattress, her fingers running through my hair. I stop to taste the skin of her stomach, kissing my way to her hipbone. "I feel so lazy."

I smile against her skin. "Not lazy—following directions."

"I thought I was the boss when we were in the bedroom?"

I stop my quest, my lips hovering inches away from her mound, my thumb so close to her pussy, I can feel the heat of it. I wait, letting the moments tick away until she lifts her head off the pillow to glare at me.

"Theodore Sutton, if you don't get that tongue of yours to work this instant, you're fired."

I grin up at her from between her thighs, exactly where I want to be. "Yes ma'am." And I get to work, delving my tongue into her sweet pussy as Sophie collapses with a shuddering moan. I alternate between licking and sucking her lips and clit, slipping my arms under her hips so I can pull her closer and bury my face in her. The sounds she makes as I taste her go straight to my cock. It's rock hard and aching, but I ignore it, needing to make Sophie come first. That doesn't stop me from grinding my own hips into the bed as I slip a finger inside her.

"Yes." Sophie moans as I work my fingers in her. Her fingers clench and tug at my hair and I groan at the pleasure that shoots down my spine from the sensation. My groan against her clit pulls a sharp gasp from her lips and her walls squeeze tight. "More, please."

"As you wi—" My words are cut off by Sophie's thighs squeezing my head and my world narrows down to the taste of her, the smell of her, the noises she makes as I tease her clit with my tongue.

"Oh God, yes!" Her words are muffled, but the desperation in them is clear—my Sunshine needs to come. I add a second finger, curling them until I find that magic spot inside her, while my tongue circles and strokes her clit. It only takes a moment before her breath hitches with a squeak, her walls clamp down on my fingers and her release spills over my chin.

I pull back, kissing the inside of each thigh as I get to my knees. Morning light peeks between the curtains, a golden line dripping across her skin. "Fuck, you're so beautiful." When she smiles at my words, her body languid and sated, the sheets tangled around us both, her golden hair splashed and mussed against the pillows, my heart twists at the perfection of it. The sight sears itself into my soul, a perfect moment, when my whole world is exactly how it's meant to be.

And then she makes it even better by reaching for me, those blue eyes full of desire. "Come here, Teddy. I need you."

Hearing her call me Teddy, no teasing, just full of need for me, rips away the last layer of protection I'd wrapped around my heart. Something desperate breaks free inside of me and I dive into her, sealing my lips to hers in a kiss. Everything I am is in that kiss—the carefully hidden man who just wants to be wanted for himself, not for what he can provide.

"Anything, everything, it's all yours, Sunshine," I murmur as I pull away, reaching for a condom.

"All I need is you." Her lips pepper my biceps and chest as I roll the condom on. Reaching between us she lines me up, before gripping my hips. I push inside her as she pulls me close, the warmth of her body and soul enveloping me with a satisfied sigh.

I start slow, reveling in her magic, letting every cell in my body rest in that feeling of being home. Home in her. The intensity of my feelings cut through the bliss Sophie's words created, startling me. I should play it safe, not get carried away. It's just a name, she can't know what hearing it does to me.

I bury my face in her neck before she can read every thought on my face. She may possess me body and soul, but I'm not ready to tell her, to give her that power over me. Instead, I pick up the pace, my slow strokes turning forceful. I graze my teeth over Sophie's shoulder. "Is this what you need?" I push my tender heart back into its cage and draw on my years of practice to keep it safe long enough to get my bearings with Sophie. "Do you need me to slam my cock into your pussy so deep you see stars?"

I unwrap one of Sophie's legs from mine and pull her thigh over my shoulder, angling to slide even deeper inside her. Using my knees for leverage, one arm beside her head, I pound into her at this angle, getting deeper with each stroke. My orgasm builds at the base of my spine. "Tell me you're close, Sunshine." I grind the words out, holding my release at bay through sheer force of will.

"Close, so close." Sophie's words are a whimper, her fingers digging into my biceps and my back. She's practically split in half beneath me, one leg pressed up against her chest, the other wrapped behind my leg, pulling me deeper inside her with each thrust. How she's so thoroughly in control when in this position is baffling, but it's true, I'm merely following the pace she's setting from beneath me. "Don't stop, Teddy."

Her words fade into a moan so deep I feel it in my stomach, her orgasm washing through her and triggering my own. I groan in response, emptying myself into the condom. The clenching of her pussy milks every last drop from me, my vision going black and stars dancing before my eyes. I suck in a breath as it clears to find a smiling Sophie grinning up at me.

Lifting my arm so she can pull her leg free, I don't roll off her just yet, enjoying the feel of her underneath me for a moment longer. "Good morning." The kiss I press to the tip of her nose turns into a series of little kisses along her cheek and forehead.

Giggling, Sophie pushes me off her. I roll to the side, pulling her to lay on my chest. "Okay, I take back my complaint. If having to share this to-die-for bed with you means I'm subjected to being woken up like that, I suppose I could get used to it." Resting her chin on my chest, she studies my face for a moment before sighing and closing her eyes again with a grimace. "We should probably get going. Real life calls."

Before she can squirm away, I hold her close. I know I need to get up and take care of the condom, and she's right, real life does call, but I can't live through another week of limbo. "It can wait another minute. Can we talk about this—about us—first?"

Sophie stills, not looking at me when she answers. "I guess."

Her tone has me on edge, the bliss of what we just shared melting away, but I need her to know that she means something to me. "Hey." I tip her chin so she has to look at me, then wrap my arms around her, holding her close. "I want this. I want more of this, more of you."

"You do?" Her hands stroking my chest go still.

"Of course I do, don't you?" I'd been sure she felt it too. "I want to take you out, show you the world."

"But what about the office?" Her chin digs into my chest as she bites her lips. "Isn't it going to be an issue? We don't have to be...um, public, if that's easier for you."

That was not what I expected to hear. "Wait, what? You think I want to keep this a secret?"

"You don't?"

"Of course not. Why would you think that, Sunshine?" A lock of her golden hair brushes against my skin. Picking it up, I twirl it between two fingers. "I'm not your supervisor. Besides, it's my goddamn company, if I want to date you I will." I can't help the force behind my words, it's the only thing hiding the fresh cracks in my heart. "Do *you* not want to be seen dating me?"

With a deep sigh, Sophie pulls free of my arms, sitting up beside me on the bed. I roll to my side so I can see her, head propped up on one arm. She wraps a sheet around her torso as she speaks, not looking me in the eye. "Theo, it's not that easy."

"I thought it was a yes or no question."

She twists some of the sheet between her fingers. "For you it is. It's so much more complicated for me." She pauses but I don't speak. "First of all, I have to think about Emma. Her dad and I just got divorced. It feels, what's the word I'm looking for?" She picks at the sheet, face scrunching as she thinks. "It feels disrespectful, I guess."

"Like the way he was disrespectful of you by cheating on you and already proposing to his new girlfriend? His new, pregnant, girlfriend?" I don't want to hurt her, but after she shared the story last weekend, I couldn't stop thinking about it. I want to murder the man.

Her shoulders hunch at my accusing words. "I know it's stupid."

Keeping my tone as measured and calm as I can, despite the fact that her yokel of an ex is still getting this much compassion from her, I touch her thigh. "Sunshine, he doesn't deserve your concern. He already proved that."

We don't speak for a long moment—Sophie looking everywhere but at me, my eyes not leaving her face. Eventually, her shoulders relax and she peeks sideways at me.

"Maybe you're right." She reaches out to smooth her hand over my cheek and into my hair. Closing my eyes I revel in the sensation. Until she clears her throat. "I wish I could say that was the only reason."

I scowl at her words and Sophie pulls away. "What's the other reason?"

Instead of answering, Sophie lays down beside me, facing me. "Can you picture it from my perspective? When word gets out at the office, you might get a few looks, but who's going to be brave enough to say anything to your face?" She traces a finger along my cheek. "But me? I'll be subject to every look, every whisper, from every Dick and Karen walking through the front door." She puts a finger over my lips before I can get a word out. "And no, moving me to a different position won't help. It will only start more gossip that I moved in the first place."

As her words sink in, I know she's right. I hate that she's right and everything in me wants to argue and fight to get my way and stop it from happening. But I can't be with her every second of the day to glare at anyone who says a word out of place.

"Hey." Her words and light tap on the nose pull me from my spiraling thoughts. "I'm not saying I don't want this." She leans forward to give me a tender kiss, pulling back before I can angle for more. "I just want to be sure before I risk everything." Her smile turns sad. "The unfortunate truth is that if things go wrong, the consequences for me are much higher than for you."

"I hate that you're right." My agreement is more of a growl, but she smiles anyway. Reaching over her waist, I pull her close before pinning her under me. Her lips are still the sweetest I've ever tasted. A buzzing from somewhere in the room, one of our phones, distracts me for a second before I dive back in for another kiss.

"Teddy, that's my phone."

"Ignore it."

She pushes me off and squirms out from under me. "At six in the morning? No can do." Without waiting for me to answer, she fishes her phone out of the pocket of her dress and looks at it, the smile on her face dropping. "Emma? Are you ok?"

Shit.

My carefree Sunshine is gone in a heartbeat, worry replacing her smile. Sophie walks into the next room, whispering frantically into the phone. I pull my own phone out of my slacks and fire off a couple of messages before picking up the hotel phone and ordering a few things.

Guess our discussion will have to wait. I slip into the bathroom and clean up as best I can, rinsing my mouth out with mouthwash and splashing water on my face before pulling on my boxers and the robe I found hanging on the back of the door. I grab an extra and toss it to Sophie just as there's a knock on the door.

Wide-eyed, she looks at me then the door, phone still pressed to her ear.

I jerk my chin toward her. "Go in the bedroom for a second."

She disappears and I pull open the door, revealing a slightly out of breath young man holding out a bag.

"Here you go, sir." His eyes go wide at the hundred dollar bill I give him before nodding and disappearing down the hall.

I take the bag inside and into the bedroom where Sophie's sitting on the edge of the bed, robe askew, still talking. "Yes, I understand...Thank you." She looks up at me with a question in her eyes.

"We can be home in two hours, maybe less." I dump the contents of the bag on the bed. I pick up the smaller of the two t-shirts and sweatpants from the gift-shop downstairs and hold them out to her. "Here. I didn't think you'd want to get dressed in *that* again." I jerk my chin at her dress laying crumpled on the floor.

She gives me a small smile before speaking back into the phone. "Yes, I give consent." She stands to take the clothes from me. "Thank you," she whispers, kissing my cheek.

"Do what you need, I'll take care of everything else," I whisper back, wishing there was more I could do. Sophie scurries into the bathroom with her clothes and phone, closing the door behind her, still on the phone.

Worried about Emma and why Sophie is consenting to things over the phone, I busy myself with gathering up all the bits of clothes we tossed around the room last night, smiling when I find my bowtie and one of her stockings hanging off the corner of the dresser. Our clothes folded and stored in the bag room service just brought, I pull on my own sweatpants and t-shirt, grimacing at the giant "Seattle, WA" logo splashed across the front. They're ugly, but much more comfortable than flying home in a wrinkled tux.

By the time Sophie emerges from the bathroom, I've gotten the text I was waiting for. "Ready? The helicopter is here."

She slips her heels back on and follows me to the door. I should have thought to have them bring her some shoes too. Next time, I won't forget.

"Thank you." There's a tremor to her voice as we head down the hallway and to the elevator. "I'm sorry for cutting everything short."

"Hey." I twine my fingers with hers as we step inside and hit the button to take us to the roof. "No apology necessary. Is Emma okay?"

Sophie turns a pair of worried eyes up to me. "I don't know. Lauren has her at the ER right now. They called so they could get started on some tests immediately. I hate that I'm so far away, that I'm not there. I'm all she has and I'm not there when she needs me." A sob bursts out of her as she finishes speaking. I try to gather her up in my arms but she turns away, hiding her face in her hands instead. "I shouldn't have come with you." Her broken words leak between her fingers with her tears.

Hand on her shoulder, I say the only thing I can think of. "This isn't your fault Sophie, you couldn't know something was going to happen."

"It doesn't matter, I shouldn't be here. I shouldn't be with you."

I don't know what cuts deeper, her words or the way she shrugs my hand off.

"You and I...it doesn't make sense."

The elevator stops, the doors slide open and the noise of the helicopter waiting for us blows my words away. "What do you mean?" I pull her back before she can step out of the elevator and conversation becomes impossible. "Sophie, what do you mean?"

My Sunshine turns to look at me with glassy eyes. "It means men like you and women like me don't belong together. We can't even be seen together in public, not without me fearing the judgment of every asshole who walks by. And you'll never understand what my life is like." She closes her eyes and a tear runs down her cheek. "This has been the most amazing fantasy, but that's all it can ever be."

She's gone, hurrying toward the helicopter before I can gather my thoughts to respond. Jogging after her, I wait to the side while the pilot helps her get in, then climb in after her.

We fly back to Portland without a word, the only things breaking the silence Sophie's muffled sniffs and my heart cracking inside my chest.

Nineteen

SOPHIE

"Mom?" Emma's voice wavers as I rush into her hospital room.

I run to her side, gripping her hand. "I'm here sweetie, I'm sorry it took me so long, but I'm here now. It's going to be okay. I got you." The relief on my baby girl's face twists my heart in my chest.

I can't believe I wasn't here when she needed me. First, her dad abandons her for his new girlfriend, then I'm off in Seattle, being seduced by my billionaire boss, drinking expensive champagne and having mind-blowing sex when she ends up in the emergency room.

"Have they done anything yet?" I'm not sure who I'm asking, Emma or Lauren, but it's Lauren who answers. How is it possible she looks cute in a pair of leggings and an oversized sweatshirt, her glasses on and hair sticking out all over?

"Just started her on a saline drip and gave her some anti-nausea and pain medication. She hasn't puked in about an hour. They were holding off on surgery until you got here since she seemed to be doing okay."

I lean down to press a kiss to Emma's head. "I'm so sorry I wasn't here. How are you feeling?"

"It still really hurts." Emma's whimper has tears pricking at my eyes. Before I can lose it completely, a doctor sticks her head in the door, knocking on the frame.

She's middle-aged, her brown hair pulled back in a low bun. She exudes competence and some of my panic eases. If anyone can explain the meaning of the universe to me, it's this woman.

"Hi, I'm Dr. Carrie Garcia. You must be Mom?" She holds her hand out and I shake it.

"Yes, I'm Emma's mom, Sophie. Is she okay? Do you know what it is?" The questions I've been dying to ask come tumbling out.

"It looks like her appendix is inflamed, we're going to need to do an emergency appendectomy."

"Surgery?" My stomach drops.

Dr. Garcia nods. "It's a routine, laparoscopic procedure. And as long as we don't encounter any complications, recovery should be pretty straightforward." I listen while Dr. Garcia explains the process to me, Lauren and Emma listening in.

A nurse appears and produces a clipboard from somewhere, going over the forms with me as Dr. Garcia talks to Emma and examines her. As soon as she's done, there's a whirlwind of nurses and people bustling around the room and then I'm squeezing my baby and kissing her forehead as they roll her away for surgery.

I gulp as I sign the line promising to pay for all treatments. Emma's covered by Jake's insurance as part of the custody agreement, and I don't know much about the policy, but I pray to any god listening that it covers everything.

I hold her hand while the nurses bustle around. "I'll be right here when you get back. I'm not going anywhere. Promise."

"Mom, stop feeling guilty, geez. I'll be fi—" Her last word ends with a groan. Clutching her stomach, Emma rolls onto her side and curls up in a ball.

A fresh wave of guilt and tears hit me at the sight. I rub her back and make soothing noises, at a loss for how to help her. A hand touches my shoulder, making me jump. "We got her." The nurse pushes me away gently, taking my place on the side of the bed. "We'll be back soon, just hang tight."

"I love you!" I call out as they wheel the bed out of the room and down the hall. I keep it together until they're gone, before collapsing against Lauren in tears.

"I can't believe I wasn't here."

Lauren doesn't say anything, just rubs my back and holds me tight while I sob.

"Stop that, no one could have known this was going to happen, Soph. She woke up and started puking at about four this morning. It's not like you abandoned her for days on end."

"But I should have been there for her." I sniff, my face already tight and puffy. "I'm her mom—I'm all she has. Instead of being with her like I should have, I was off having amazing sex and being swept off my feet!"

"Okay, first of all we're going to discuss that last sentence, in detail, later. Second of all, you're *not* all she has. What am I? Chopped liver? If we hadn't been able to get hold of you, I would have called Jake again. He didn't pick up the first time, and he didn't respond to my text, but I'm sure he would have come if I called enough times." Lauren gives me a little shake. "Now, knock it off with the mom guilt. It could have happened even if you were in town and she was sleeping over at Bella's house or something."

Lauren's sensible words settle in my mind. The guilt over being with Theo doesn't leave, but it pauses hammering away at my brain. I suck in a shaky breath, snot and tears adding a disgusting touch to the sound. "Oh gross." Spying a box of tissues on a countertop nearby, I pull out a few and sort out my face. "What made you decide to bring her?"

Lauren shakes her head, joining me at the counter to steal a tissue of her own. "It wasn't so much because of the uncontrollable puking, but because she was complaining about her stomach feeling like someone was stabbing her, and she has a fever. Plus, I remembered how she got car sick on the drive to my house."

"She got carsick? Emma never gets carsick."

Lauren bumps me with her hip. "Exactly. She was pretty subdued last night and didn't eat a lot. I thought maybe there was something going on with her friends and was trying to see if she'd talk to me, but I think she just wasn't feeling good."

With nothing to do but wait, we lapse into silence. Memories of last night, and this morning, compete with worry for Emma in my head. What must Theo think of me now? I know he said he wanted more of this, but I don't think he really knew what he was signing up for. I'm not one of the young, carefree model-types he's been seen with before. I come with baggage.

Not just any baggage. A teenager. A shitty ex-husband. My own insecurities. He's smart enough to figure out that he should be running away from me as fast as those long, muscular legs can carry him.

Those legs. And that ass.

I hadn't been able to keep my hands off that tight, firm ass of his last night.

I am the world's worst mother, sitting here fantasizing about my boss's bite-worthy derriere while my kid is having surgery. With a groan, I bury my face in Lauren's shoulder.

"What's up, buttercup?" The shoulder I'm leaning on shifts and Lauren pulls me close, pressing a kiss to the top of my head. "Thinking about all that hot sex you had last night?"

A cross between a laugh and a sob escapes me. "You're sworn to secrecy, but ugh, it was so good. It was Lucy Score-level hot." Lauren snorts at my description. "I think all those articles about his genius must be wrong though."

"Why do you say that?"

"There has to be something wrong with his brain because he said he wants to date me."

Lauren stiffens. "Sophie. For the love of every romance novel we've ever read, tell me you said yes." When I don't answer she pulls away, forcing me to look at her face. "You said yes, right? I swear woman, if you said no I will steal your signed copy of *Outlander*."

With a sigh, I pick at the lettering printed down the leg of my sweatpants. "I thanked him for an incredible evening, but told him that in reality it would never work." Lauren's groan has my shoulders creeping up towards my ears. "My life isn't a billionaire romance, Lauren. This is the real world, my actual life. I'm not living out some 'grumpy one is soft for the sunshine one' trope."

"Pretty sure *you're* the grumpy one in this story." Lauren leans back in her chair, arms crossed over her chest.

I mimic her, my fingers twisting in my lap instead. "You're calling the Bastard-in-Chief the sunshine one?" But I know she's right. Even calling him by our old nickname makes my stomach twist uncomfortably, now that I know it's all an act. The armor he wears to run his company. I've seen the tender heart he hides behind the grumpy persona.

Before Lauren can respond, there's a buzz from my purse. Pulling out my phone, expecting to see a message from Jake, what I'm greeted with is just one more illustration of the thoughtful man who runs Mailbox with an iron fist.

Tall, Dark and Handsome: *There's a delivery for you at the emergency room reception. I'm not asking for anything, I just need to know you're being taken care of.*

Lauren grins, reading over my shoulder. "You stay here, I'll go get it."

"Lauren, no. I told him we weren't dating. I can't accept whatever it is he sent."

The sting of Lauren's loving smack to the back of my head is the only response I get. She's out of the room and down the hall before I can stop her, leaving me to stew over what Teddy could have sent.

Me: *That wasn't necessary.*

Tall, Dark and Handsome: *You don't even know what it is yet. Maybe I sent you a stack of files to go through.*

Me: *That's not even my job. Lauren went to get it.*

Tall, Dark and Handsome: *Yes, I know. Ms. Masterson, at least, was properly receptive to the delivery.*

He's here? He brought it himself?

Me: *Why are you being so thoughtful?*

Tall, Dark and Handsome: *Why wouldn't I be?*

That's an excellent question. I just didn't expect that a man who could have anything, or anyone he wanted, would take the time to look after me. I'm not special. I'm not a genius like him. I'm pretty enough, but I'm not a bombshell. I'm just average. It never would have occurred to Jake to do something like this unless I asked.

Lauren comes back into the room carrying a cardboard tray, two coffee cups stuck in it with a brown paper bag between them. The scent of fresh, hot coffee and some kind of pastry tickles my nose. "Girl, if you don't want him, can I have him?"

"No." The word is out my mouth before I can think, earning me a knowing wink.

"Thank the man. And don't think I didn't notice the matching t-shirt/sweatpants combo you two have going on." She opens the bag and hands me a cheese danish. Of course he remembered.

Me: *Thank you for the coffee and danish.*

Tall, Dark and Handsome: *Least I could do. How's Emma?*

Me: *She has to have an emergency appendectomy. They just took her in.*

Tall, Dark and Handsome: *If you need anything let me know.*

What I need is a million dollars and double the amount of hours in the day, but a kind word is good too.

We've been waiting about forty-five minutes when Jake comes strolling into the room.

"Nice of you to show up." Lauren's sarcastic remark pulls me from the exhausted whirlwind of my thoughts.

A heavy hand settles on my shoulder. "Fuck you too, Lauren." Jake squeezes my shoulder, the familiar gesture no longer bringing me comfort the way it used to. It used to feel like he was giving me a mini hug when he did that, now it's just one more reminder that I spent the last sixteen years with this excuse for a man, dragging him along through life. "Any word?"

Maybe it's because I'm sleep-deprived, maybe it's because I'm sick with worry, but I can't stop myself from snapping back at him. "Oh, now you care? Where have you been for the last few hours, huh?" I twist to look up at him, knocking his hand off me. "Your daughter was in pain and in the E.R. and you only bothered to show up now?"

Jake's face turns hard. "Some of us have responsibilities. I couldn't just leave Kasidee the second Lauren texted. Besides, it's not like Emma needed me, she had you."

Slumping back in my chair in defeat, I swallow my words. He's right, I've always been the one to take care of Emma, to put her needs before mine. Since I was pregnant and struggling to finish my college classes—I've put her first, unlike Jake. Even though I was the one to actually graduate and he dropped out, it wasn't to get a job like he claims. He was already failing his classes and in danger of being kicked out before we even found out Emma was on the way. Our courthouse wedding so he could "do the right thing" was his excuse to quit before anyone found out.

Why would I expect anything to change, especially now that we're divorced?

"Do you hear yourself?" Lauren's question infiltrates the guilt eating at me. "Your *daughter* is in the hospital and you didn't feel a need to be here because Sophie would? Did it ever occur to you that Sophie might not enjoy the responsibility of dealing with all of your shit? And that Emma might want you here to show that you actually care about her? For fucks's sake, Jake."

"Whatever, Lauren. Thank Christ I don't have to deal with your shit anymore. It was like being married to both of you. The Harpy and the Shrew." Jake's shudder of disgust sends another wave of guilt through me. Had my friendship with Lauren really been such an issue? Had I ruined our marriage because I'd been leaning on Lauren for the support Jake didn't give me?

The sound of metal wheels and creaking plastic has me on my feet and peeking down the corridor, ignoring the argument heating up between Jake and Lauren. I can't tell if the lump on the hospital bed making its way towards me is my Emma or not. When the nurses turn to bring her inside the room, I scoot out of the way while they wheel her in.

Jake and Lauren's bickering doesn't matter—I only have eyes and ears for my daughter and Doctor Garcia. The argument has wound down by the time the nurses and doctor leave us with a sleeping Emma. I stroke her hair and watch for signs of her waking, my phone clutched in my hand for security. The buzz of a text coming through startles me from my reverie.

> *Tall, Dark and Handsome: Is she still in surgery? What can I do to help?*

The smile that creeps across my face is equal parts relief that Emma's going to be okay, and excitement at the very handsome man whose bed I was in last night.

> *Me: Just got out. Everything went smoothly. Thank you for offering, but we're good.*

Looking up at the man I'd been married to since I was barely twenty, who hasn't asked if I needed anything for years, who was just one more weight for me to drag through life, I can't believe I ever fell for his crap. I would have been better off raising Emma on my own than shackling us both to his dead weight.

And there's another reason why Theo can only ever be a fantasy. I'm not willing to give up my chance to be free. Was it an amazing weekend? Absolutely. But it's going to take a lot more than a weekend of amazing sex to make me hand over control of my life again.

Twenty

THEO

FLIPPING BETWEEN TABS, I debate between sending an edible fruit arrangement, a unicorn onesie, or a collection of baked goods from the bakery down the street. Sophie hasn't been at work for the last two days, understandably, and I've been assuaging my need to see her by sending gifts to her and Emma.

Yesterday's pack of fuzzy socks and flowers led to a dozen texts between Sophie and I. I pull out my phone and reread them while I debate how mad she'd be if I sent all three.

> **Sunshine:** *Thank you for the sock collection, it was very sweet of you to send it, even if it was wholly unnecessary.*

This had been accompanied by a photo of her and Emma's feet on a bed, each foot wearing a different one of the socks I'd sent. I don't have a foot fetish, but the sight of the two of them wearing something I'd sent had my squishy heart turning over in my chest.

> **Me:** *I just wanted to make sure Emma's recovery wasn't hindered by having cold toes. Hers or yours. I'd hate for you to develop cold feet.*

> **Sunshine:** *... I see what you're doing. I don't have cold feet. How can you have cold feet when there's nothing to run away from? I already told you, things between us can't go any further than they already have.*

> **Me:** *And yet, I can't stop thinking about you Sunshine.*

She hasn't answered that text and it's been driving me crazy.

The women I've dated in the past asked me to pay for clothes, vacations, hell, one of them asked me to pay her rent on the third date and we hadn't even kissed. But not Sophie. I'm debating between a twenty-dollar onesie and a forty-dollar fruit arrangement because I have a suspicion that if I send both she'll yell at me and won't let me send anything else. I could buy her anything she wanted, but she won't accept it.

Annoyed that she won't ask for anything, I arrange for the onesie to be delivered now, the fruit basket this afternoon and the pastries in the morning. My email inbox chimes with incoming messages for me to wade through so I finish setting up the deliveries and force myself to stop thinking about Sunshine and focus on my company.

Hours later, I'm entrenched in an exchange with one of the software engineers when a new incoming email catches my eye. It's an application to the employee assistance program I set up. Officially, the program is sponsored by Mailbox and employees have the option of contributing to it with each paycheck. In return, they can ask for a scholarship from the fund if need arises. In reality, all their contributions are invested by the fund to earn interest, and I personally cover the costs of most requests to it. Contributors get their money back in the form of an additional annual bonus. There aren't usually many requests for assistance and the ones we do get tend to be pretty small. I make sure that we pay our employees well with excellent insurance benefits.

I click over to the request, fingers crossed that it's not another dog with cancer—there were two of those last quarter and it broke my heart both times. The first line of the request has not only my heart breaking, but my blood boiling. It's from Sophie. For fifteen-thousand dollars. Which, thanks to some snooping and a conversation with Ms. Masterson, I happen to know is half the amount she owes the hospital for Emma's appendectomy.

I stare at the request. Why would she need so much money? Shouldn't our insurance cover most of it? And why is she asking for it from the employee fund and not from me?

"Mr. Sutton?" Mercedes sticks her head in my door. "Are you alright? I can hear you muttering out here." Her glasses are perched on the end of her nose, eyeing me over the edge like one of her wayward grandchildren. "While I'm here, I'm going to point out that it's almost four o'clock and you haven't had lunch yet."

I wave away the suggestion of food. "Is there a way I can check to see if an employee is utilizing our health insurance?"

Mercedes cocks her head. "Is there something I can help you with?" Before I can formulate an answer, she continues. "Does it have something to do with Ms. Alexander?"

I scrape my fingers through my hair, face scrunched in annoyance. "How do you...I mean. What?" God, Casey really did inherit every ounce of acting ability in our family. "Why would it have anything to do with her?"

Mercedes steps all the way into my office, closing the door behind her. "Sir, may I speak freely?"

"Of course."

"I've seen the way you look at her, the way you are so careful not to single her out." At my scowl, Mercedes continues. "I also saw the assistance request come in and it wasn't difficult to put two and two together. You know more about her personal life than you're letting on."

The way she's staring me down, one eyebrow raised, fills me with an urge to squirm in my chair like she caught me with my hand in the candy jar. "Her daughter had to have emergency surgery over the weekend." I explain. "I just don't understand why she needs so much money for the hospital bill if our insurance should be covering it. Do I need to look into our coverage? Or is there something else going on?"

"There's a very simple way to find out, Mr. Sutton." When I don't answer, she shakes her head. "You could just *ask* her."

Why doesn't it feel that simple?

Sunshine: *I told you we don't need anything else. I'm going to let the next delivery driver keep whatever it is you've sent this time.*

Sophie's text comes through right before she flings the door open. "Oh!" Her eyes go wide at the sight of me. "I thought...I just assumed." She stumbles back a step, glancing behind her with a grimace. "Theo, now's not a good time."

Ignoring her protest, I step inside her tiny apartment. This is where they live? It's the size of my kitchen. Looking around, I take in the pillows and blanket on the couch, as if someone's been sleeping there, the take-out containers in the trash and her pajama-clad state. There are dark circles under her eyes and her hair looks like it's been piled on top of her head for days on end.

"Theo. Mr. Sutton. Please, it's not a good time." Sophie's whispering and trying to block me from coming further inside with her tiny body.

I tear my gaze away from the tiny, disheveled apartment to look her in the eye. "Sophie, I just wanted to make sure you and Emma were okay. And see if you need anything."

She steps outside, shutting the door gently behind her. "We're fine, like I said. We don't need anything."

I open my mouth to speak but Sophie steamrolls right over me. "Theo, you have to stop. You have to stop sending things. I don't want..." She glances back at the apartment behind her. "I don't want Emma to get the wrong idea. It's my problem, not yours. I can take care of it."

Irritation that she won't just take my goddamn help surges through me. "So you'd rather live in squalor, rather ask for anonymous help than ask me?"

The second the words leave my lips, I know I've said the wrong thing. "Squalor?" Her face turns bright red and I can almost see the steam coming out of her ears. "It's small and a little messy, but it's not dirty. This is a nice apartment, you asshole." She shoves at my chest but I plant my feet and refuse to be budged. "Just because I don't live in a mansion like you, with a ridiculous shower doesn't mean I live in a dump!"

"I thought you liked my shower?" I don't bother to hide the smirk on my face at the memory of her in my shower, the way she'd sank to her knees in there, water hitting us from all sides.

"Ugh!" Stepping away from her door, she pokes a finger into my chest with a growl of frustration. Hard enough to hurt a little. I probably shouldn't antagonize her, but I can't seem to stop myself. "You are such a...such a *man*. I am asking you to stop sending things. I told you, I can't accept them."

"Can't or won't?"

Sophie sighs, some of the fight going out of her. "Won't. I told you, this thing between us isn't meant to be. You can't just throw money and gifts at me and expect it to solve everything. I'll be back at work on Monday." She steps back, hand on the door behind her. A sad smile graces her lips and I want to kiss it away. "I'm sorry."

She's through the door and locking it before I can speak, my voice gone and throat dry.

Shoving my hands in my pockets, I tear myself away from the door and head to my car. It takes the entire two-mile drive before my thoughts are clear enough for her words to sink in.

She doesn't want my help. She doesn't want me.

Twenty-one

SOPHIE

"I LOOK OKAY, RIGHT?" I tug at my pencil skirt, an awkward move when perched half on a bar stool.

"You look amazing, Soph. Stop fidgeting." Lauren's bright red lips close around the straw in her drink before sucking down a long draw of her vodka soda.

Picking up my tumbler, I copy her, the bite of my drink distracting me from feeling self-conscious about my sheer top and tight skirt. "Why are we here again?"

"Because you need to forget about Jake and Theo and *live* a little." Lauren raises one penciled eyebrow at me. "Also, Emma begged me to take you out. You're smothering her."

"She just had emergency surgery, of course I'm smothering her. And I don't need to forget about Theo. There's nothing to be sad about."

Lauren doesn't answer, just stares at me while she takes a long drink.

"I did the right thing, Lauren. He lives in a completely different world to me."

Silence.

"Stop judging me. I'm not *that* girl, I don't take handouts from rich men."

That gets me a snort and a response. "When have you ever been offered a handout by a rich man? Jake sucked every penny you earned since we were college sophomores."

"You know what I mean. I'm not..." My fuzzy brain won't offer up the word I want. "I'm not so desperate that I..." I don't finish that sentence because it would be a lie. I am that desperate, hence why Lauren is acting as my sugar-mama on this night out. Every time I try to buy a round, she won't let me.

We've been here long enough for a couple of drinks and four different guys to hit on Lauren. Being a good friend, she's turned them all down, staying with me while I wallow in misery. But even two drinks in, I can tell she's losing patience with me.

I'm not supposed to be miserable—I had every reason to turn Teddy down. All those reasons feel hollow now, when I'm sad and lonely and want nothing more than to feel his arms wrapped around my waist. "He wants to just buy me. He can't just buy me like that."

Lauren pats my knee while rolling her eyes. "He's not trying to *buy* you, he's trying to take care of you. Jesus Christ, woman. I love you, but you are so fucking stubborn."

I huff. "I am not."

"You are." Lauren sticks her tongue out. "You won't let me help pay for Emma's hospital bill, and you won't let Theo help you. Jake can't help since him being out of work again is the reason Emma was uninsured. But *you* can't pay it either. I know you don't have thirty thousand dollars laying around, babe. What other option is there?"

I shake my head, unwilling to hear her point. "I'll figure it out."

Lauren stares over the edge of her glass. "How?"

"I don't know." I shrug. "But I'll figure it out. I don't need anyone's help."

"God, you are infuriating sometimes." With a snort, she sets her glass down on the bar. "Let me know when you're ready to be reasonable and have an actual adult conversation about this." She stalks off to the dance floor before I can respond.

Fuzzy-brained, I stare as she slips into the crowd. The bar she dragged me to is not a place I would normally go, the crowd of well-dressed and lithe bodies too hip for my comfort.

A tall, dark-haired man in ripped jeans and a leather jacket moves behind her, his hips slowing to match hers. I'm mesmerized by the way he snakes a hand along her hip to splay across her stomach, pulling her against him as they dance. I can feel the ghost of Teddy's hands on me the same way.

Closing my eyes, I let the thumping bass saturate my bones. I want to kick myself for falling into Teddy's bed like I did. For years I hadn't needed that kind of touch, hadn't needed to feel a man's hands on my body. I'd pushed away my desire to feel wanted until I could ignore it.

And then Teddy went and lit a fire in me that I can't extinguish.

I want to hate him, but I can't. Lauren is right. He's not trying to buy me, he's just trying to help. Same as she is. But the idea of taking their money rankles.

"Hey sweet cheeks, did you want another?" The bartender who's been pouring our drinks all night raps his knuckles on the bar top to get my attention. I nod, slurping down the last of my drink. "Still on your friend's tab?"

I'm so tired of being the poor friend. The one who needs help. I want to be able to pay my own way. I don't need an extravagant life—I don't need millions. I want to be able to go grocery shopping without calculating the total and praying I have enough in the bank to cover it.

"No, put this one on mine." I fish in my clutch for the card I'd stuffed in there earlier. He takes it and proceeds to pour another delicious concoction of whiskey and other stuff into a shaker for me. "What am I drinking? I forgot."

The deep voice and warm body that slides in behind me should startle me. "Looks like a whiskey sour to me." If I wasn't two drinks deep, it would have. Instead, I let a smile creep across my face and swivel to face the speaker.

He's taller than I expected and lean. His sharp features give him an aristocratic air. I suppose he would be considered attractive, although his visibly thinning dirty-blond hair is too long for my taste. But I smile anyway. This is good, I should practice this kind of thing.

"That sounds right. Are you an expert?" My words are fuzzy round the edges, but I pair them with an attempt at a flirtatious smile. I haven't been hit on since I was in college and I forgot what a boost it could be to my self-confidence.

"I don't know if I'd say I was an *expert*, but I've had my fair share of them." He leans close, his next words buzzing against my ear. "Are you here alone?"

I pull back and point to Lauren, still dancing in the crowd. "No, I'm here with my friend."

"You don't want to dance?" He rests a hand on my shoulder, his thumb tracing circles against my skin. If it was Teddy, I'd be purring like a cat at the touch. But mystery man's caress isn't doing anything for me. Is it awful that I want to shrug him off?

"I like to dance. I just haven't felt like it yet." I shrug, hoping it'll knock his hand off me. It doesn't, but he lets go to take my drink from the bartender and slide it over.

I pick it up to take a sip, the sweet and sour liquid burning as it hits my throat.

"Did you want to leave it open or close the tab?"

I swipe my hand across my throat to tell the bartender to close my tab and he disappears to the terminal a few feet away.

"What's your name?" Blondie asks, leaning close to me to be heard over the music. I'm pretty sure he also took a peek down my cleavage. Teddy would have been more subtle.

"Elinor." Being Elinor is more fun than being Sophie. My whiskey-soaked brain agrees with me. "What's yours?"

"Danny. You want to dance?"

I slurp down more of my drink, letting it tell me that dancing with a random man is a great idea.

What better way to get over Teddy than to dance the night away with some guy who hit on me in a random bar? Besides, Danny obviously thinks I'm attractive. Maybe this is just the boost I need to forget my regret over turning Teddy down and live a little. Isn't that what Lauren is always telling me?

I'm about to swivel away from the bar to go dance, when I remember I need my card. The bartender is making his way back, a concerned scowl on his face, my card in his hand. "Sorry Doll, your card keeps being declined. Do you have cash or do you want me to go ahead and put the drink on your friend's tab?"

And just like that, my bubble bursts.

"You can put it on my tab," Danny says before I can answer. "I was going to offer to buy this beautiful lady a drink anyway."

My stomach hollows out. Saved once again by the kindness of a stranger. I can't even afford to buy myself a fucking drink. Anger and humiliation burn through me, leaving me shaking and on the verge of tears.

He turns to me and holds out a hand. "Come on."

I finish my drink and set the empty glass on the bar top. "Thank you. You didn't have to do that." I have to pull him down to shout in his ear. I don't meet his eyes, too humiliated that he heard what happened.

Danny runs a hand up my back, guiding me onto the dance floor. "I was going to anyway, in the hopes I'd get you to come dance with me."

I let him lead me out onto the floor, passing Lauren with a brush against her arm so she sees me.

I still haven't met his eyes, but I let him pull me close, his warm hand spread against my back. The music settles in my body and my hips sway from side to side with the beat, Danny matching me. I reach my arms up to rest them on his shoulders, my eyes drifting closed as we dance. For a second, I expect to feel Teddy's solid shoulders under my arms, anticipating the muscled form I've learned over the last few weeks. Danny's smaller frame takes me by surprise and I pull back.

To cover up my movement, I take his hand and turn underneath it, pressing my back to his chest instead. Maybe if I don't have to look at him I can pretend I'm enjoying myself.

Grateful that the music is too loud to talk, I sway with the beat, my mind racing.

How can I afford to pay for Emma's hospital bill?

I can't reduce my expenses—there's nothing to cut back. I buy the bare minimum of groceries to feed us, and we don't splurge on extras.

The only real option is to make more money. I've always turned down the offers from various managers at Mailbox to steal me away from my position, not wanting to take on a job that would require more overtime or responsibility. With Jake's income added to mine, I hadn't needed the extra money so badly that it had been worth giving up my writing and mom time.

And if I'm being perfectly honest, I had been too scared of failure at a different kind of job to pursue it. I'm good at my position. Excellent, even. So what if there's no real opportunity to make more money there. It's safe. Just like staying with Jake, as unhappy as we were, was safe.

Jesus Christ, why am I like this?

Why am I so scared of putting myself out there?

I am a total fucking coward.

My throat tightens and I know that tears are imminent. The humiliation of not being able to pay for my drink, combined with the self-loathing brought on by my alcohol-induced introspection, is sending me into the depths of helplessness.

I can't stop the crying I know is about to happen. The only thing I can do is let it wash over me and pray that Danny doesn't turn me around until I can get it under control.

So I stop fighting it. I let the tears well up and flow down my cheeks, still dancing. Danny's hands are roaming over me, skating along my sides and hips. His thumb brushes against the underside of my breast and fresh tears trickle down.

This was not the life I wanted.

Humiliated.

Lonely.

So desperate for distraction that I'm dancing with a man I feel nothing for, rather than let the man I want take care of me.

Lauren swings by but doesn't notice my tears, probably because the guy she's dancing with has his lips locked with hers. I'm not mad, this is my own fault. I could have pursued a better-paying job months ago when I first left Jake. I should have checked to make sure that Emma's health insurance was still up to date, not trusted Jake to be on top of it.

I shouldn't have pushed Teddy away.

The tears aren't stopping. In fact, the thought of Teddy's crestfallen face when I turned down his help has them coming harder and faster until I can't pretend anymore and I stop dancing, a sob escaping me.

"Whoa, are you okay?" Danny's concern only makes me cry harder.

I shake my head and push away from him, aiming for the doors of the club. Someone catches my elbow, stopping me.

"Soph, what's wrong?" Lauren's face is scrunched with worry. "Did someone hurt you? Who was it? Was it that creepy guy?" I can't do anything but shake my head, my throat too thick to speak.

"He's fine." I manage to get out between hiccups. "I just need to go home."

"You can't go home like that, you'll scare Emma." Lauren steers me toward a table by the door. "Wait here while I close my tab. I'll be right back."

I swipe a napkin off the table, then lean against the edge, wiping my eyes and attempting to calm down. I keep my eyes down, not wanting to know how many people are staring at the old woman who came to the club and cried on the dancefloor.

"Are you okay?" Danny's loafers step into my line of sight. "You scared me."

I shake my head. "I'm sorry, it's not you. I'm a mess tonight."

He reaches out to touch my arm, startling me into looking up. "I'm sorry if I did anything that was inappropriate or..."

"No, no." I interrupt him. "You didn't do anything wrong. I just need to go home and get my life sorted out. I had an epiphany on the dance floor, nothing to do with you."

"What kind of epiphany?" He raises an eyebrow, head cocked to the side. He's really not an unattractive man. If I'd met him in another life, I could be attracted to him. But he's not Teddy. And I don't have the time or energy in my life to invest in a relationship.

"The kind where I realize I can't keep on going like I am."

Lauren shoulders her way between us, giving Danny a dirty look. "You ready?"

Am I ready to start taking charge of my life? For real this time, not just reacting to things I can't control?

"Yeah. I'm ready."

Twenty-two

THEO

"DID WE GET A particularly useless batch of interns, or is it just me?" I don't even have to pretend to be an asshole. The black hole Sophie ripped in my chest has swallowed up every ounce of good-nature I possess. And to make matters worse, she didn't return to work on Monday like she said she would. It's Thursday and I haven't seen a trace of her. How am I supposed to get anything done when she's not here?

No one answers. A conference room packed full of software developers and not a single one speaks up. Probably for the best, I don't want an answer.

"Someone get me a working pen." I growl, tossing the useless dry erase marker on the table, letting it roll across the wooden surface. It hits someone's mug and spins off onto the floor, a soft thump as it hits the carpet echoing in the silent room.

All the engineers freeze, eyes wide, before a mad scramble ensues, hands patting pockets and digging through purses to find me a new pen. Ignoring them, I turn back to the white board where I was outlining the software I started developing, the one inspired by Sophie's conversation with the head of IT at the hospital.

Embedding the notes and videos into each case file wasn't the problem, the problem is that now I want to figure out how to allow the doctors or nurses to make notes directly in the video file itself. If teenagers on social media can do it, why can't we?

"Mr. Sutton?"

"What?" It's more bark than word. I turn from the whiteboard to find myself face to face with the newest software developer on our staff. Frankie Emory is a wisp of a thing, her big brown eyes wide and fearful as I turn the full force of my bad mood on her.

"H-h-here." She thrusts a dry erase marker at me before scurrying away to sit in the chair furthest from me. Fuck. The new girl didn't deserve that. Guilt gnaws at me when I catch her scooting her chair into the shadow of the older dev sitting next to her.

Derek turns to speak to her, shooting me a cautious look over his shoulder after she responds too quietly for me to hear. The guilt turns into full-fledged regret over my actions. I know I've cultivated a reputation for being an asshole, but I've never laid into anyone who hadn't deserved it. Until now.

If Sophie was here, I know exactly what she'd say. *Really Teddy? Is being an asshole doing anyone any good? Are they actually paying attention, or are they so scared you'll fire one of them in a fit of rage that they're just praying for it to be over? Is this making you feel any better?*

The growling helps, but that's not respect in their eyes as they stare up at me from the table. It's fear.

And it's not making me feel any better.

"You know what? I think we're good for now. If everyone could go ahead and start working on what we've got, maybe do some brainstorming on your own, I'll have Mercedes schedule another meeting when I get back." I nod to Mercedes, knowing she'll take care of the follow up, and stride from the room.

Back in my office, I'm halfway through booking myself a flight to California when Mercedes sticks her head in. "Sir? Where exactly are you going? And when will you be back?"

I glare at her. She glares right back.

"You have a meeting with Mr. Edwards tomorrow at ten that I'll need to reschedule." Her reminder that I can't just up and walk away from everything isn't helping my mood, but she's right.

Rubbing my temples, I slump back in my chair. "I'm going to go visit my sister and her kids. I'll be back in a week...ish." I have to get out of here. Every time I walk past that desk and Sophie isn't there, my heart cracks just a little more. Hiding it behind my asshole persona just isn't enough anymore, not now that I've had a taste of her.

"Sir?"

I look up, surprised that Mercedes is still there. "Yes?"

She leans back, looking around, before stepping inside my office and shutting the door behind her, then crossing to my desk and sitting down in a chair. "You better not be giving up."

"Giving up? On what?"

Mercedes just raises an eyebrow at me. "What did I say about the soap?" She pauses, letting her words sink in. "You've been happier in the last three weeks than I've ever seen you. She's good for you."

I shake my head, not bothering to deny her words. "That's not the problem Mercedes. She's the best thing that's ever happened to me. But she doesn't feel the same way. She won't let me in, won't let me help. Every time I offer, she pushes me away."

"She's divorced, right? A single mom to a teenager. How long has she been struggling? How long has she carried the weight of supporting herself and her daughter without any help?"

Details that Sophie's shared with me about her ex-husband have a growl building in my chest. "Always. She's always been the one carrying the load, as far as I can tell. Her ex could never keep a steady job, and was always spending their money pursuing his hobbies." I shove a hand through my hair, tugging at it in irritation. "Which is why I don't understand why she won't let me help her. Isn't she exhausted? Doesn't she *want* help?"

Mercedes doesn't answer right away. I finish booking my flight and email the itinerary to my sister while I wait. If seeing Casey, Clara, and Ethan doesn't help, I don't know what will.

"Maybe she's scared of letting you take away any of her burden, in case you decide to give it back to her." Her words are clear in the quiet of my office.

"Give it back to her?"

"If she allows you to help, gets used to you being there and sharing her burdens—what happens to her if things go bad? You? You'll be heartbroken, like you are now, but in the end you'll be fine. You'll have a roof over your head, a nice car to drive, and someone else to stock your fridge full of fresh food whether she's there or not."

I lean my elbows on the desk, opening my mouth to protest, but Mercedes cuts me off.

"It'll be a sad and lonely life, and that comes with it's own problems, but not a hard one."

I can't deny the truth of that statement. It doesn't mean I want that life though. The memory of Emma wandering into my house, her muffled exclamations over how nice it is, how big it is, while I'd stared dumbfounded at Sophie, rush back to me.

Before, I'd thought it was adorable. The idea of introducing Emma and Sophie to my lifestyle. I admit to myself I'd had fantasies of taking them shopping, letting them buy anything and everything they wanted. "What's wrong with wanting to make someone else's life a little easier?"

"Nothing, sir. Offering help to those who need it is never a bad thing." Mercedes is quick to respond. "But giving a hand up to an employee who needs it, is very different to stealing away someone's burden's and leaving them wondering when they're going to have to take it back from you. The uncertainty is exhausting."

I eye my assistant. "It sounds like you're speaking from experience."

She laughs. "That's because I am." When I don't say anything she pats my hand on the desk and continues. "Do you know what HR told me on my first day as your assistant? They wished me luck and urged me to stay at least three weeks since that's how long it would take to find a replacement for me."

"What?" I knock a pile of papers across my desk as I jerk back.

Mercedes grabs the stack and shuffles it back together. "Oh, they were perfectly nice about it. But do you remember how many assistants you went through before me?"

I shake my head. Before Mercedes, my assistants had been a blur of useless or incompetent college graduates. I guess there were a lot of them.

"You hadn't had an assistant last longer than three months when I started here. You either fired them, or they left in tears. But that's not the point."

"What is the point then? Besides reminding me that I'm a grumpy old monster of a boss?"

"The point, sir, is that I spent the first six months of this job terrified that you were going to fire me. I was making the most money I'd ever made in my life, but I tossed and turned in my bed every night. I was finally able to catch up on all the late bills that had been keeping me up before you hired me, but I was sure everyday was going to be my last. I could pay off debts, and still have enough to buy myself whatever I wanted..." She pauses, blinking back tears. "Yet, I couldn't sleep at night because I was so scared this was going to be ripped away from me on your whim."

Offended, I sputter. "But—"

Mercedes stops me with a shake of her head. "It's not that *you* are the problem, sir. The problem is that when you've been in survival mode for that long, your instinct is not to trust any help that's offered to you—because in the end it doesn't last. And a taste of that kind of peace, then losing it, is worse than never having tasted it at all."

She pats me on the hand once more as she stands. "Have a good time with Casey and the kids, I'll hold the fort while you're gone. And don't you dare give up on Sophie."

"But what if she's given up on me?"

"She hasn't, but she's scared. Stop cornering the poor girl and let her take the lead."

Ethan and I lean back against the couch to admire our handiwork, the multi-colored tower of Lego blocks wobbling precariously when his foot kicks the coffee table leg in his haste to scoot closer to me. "Nicely done, my man." I offer my hand for a high five and he slaps it as hard as his six-year-old self can. Which is surprisingly hard.

Laughing, I rub my stinging palm on my leg. "Will you take a picture to send to my dad?" His dark eyes are big and pleading, as if I could possibly say no to him.

In answer, I pull out my phone and snap a picture. "Go hop up and stand next to it, so he can see how tall it is." I snap another photo of Ethan standing proudly next to our tower, his hand held up above it, and text it to Garrett. Ethan wanted to see if we could make one as tall as he is. Luckily, the coffee table helped us make up the last foot of distance.

> **Me:** *Ethan wanted to make a tower as tall as he is. You're gonna have to spend another few thousand dollars on more Lego if he's going to be able to do it again in six months. How is he so tall already?*

I pocket my phone, not expecting an answer right away, not when Garrett is busy shooting.

"Uncle Teddy, can we watch TV?" The tower forgotten, Ethan is halfway out the room before I can corral him back.

I point to the tower. "We gotta clean up first. Remember what happened last night?"

At my reminder of last night's drama, Ethan's face scrunches. "Oh. Yeah." He looks around the spacious living room with its airy ceilings and mostly white and gray furniture. "Can you hold the box? I'll smash the tower." He grins at that.

Grateful to skip a repeat of last night's tears over not being able to watch cartoons before bed, I hold the box while Ethan proceeds to Hulk-smash his way through taking apart the tower we spent the last hour building. I'm helping him snap the lid on top of the giant plastic storage container when Casey wanders back into the living room, baby monitor clipped to her pants.

"Mommy! We cleaned up. Can I watch TV with Uncle Teddy?" Ethan throws himself at her legs, wrapping his arms around my sister's hips and staring up at her from below her belly button.

"Good job cleaning up, buddy. You can go watch one episode but then it's time for bed." Casey ruffles his hair and something twists in my chest at the sight. She may complain about the kids being a handful, but I know she's happier now than she's ever been.

Half an hour and a nonsensical cartoon later, Ethan hops up from his spot cuddled into my side on the couch. "Night, Uncle Teddy." He's out of the room in a flash, swinging on the doorway as he rounds the corner.

Pulling out my phone, I unlock it, hoping for some kind of message. I'm not really sure what I'm looking for, just some kind of acknowledgement that I matter to someone outside of work. Without anyone to respond to, I scroll lazily through my various social media apps, killing time.

"Who's that? She's gorgeous?" Casey says, plopping onto the couch next to me.

"That's our Content Editor, Lauren Masterson." I clear my throat. "She's, uh, Sophie's best friend."

Casey snatches my phone out of my hand. "Oooo, are we stalking her to find pictures of the elusive Sophie? Let me see." She scrolls for a moment before handing the phone back with a disappointed look on her face. "You can do better than this, genius hacker little bro. Where's the good stuff?"

I chuckle at her teasing even as a weight settles in the pit of my stomach. "What's the point Case? She doesn't want me. I came out here to get over her, not indulge your voyeuristic tendencies."

"Why are you trying to get over her? I thought you wanted to try to win her over?" She holds my phone out of reach when I make a grab for it.

"She told me to leave her alone. I don't want to be *that* guy." I growl, crossing my arms and slumping back into the couch cushions. "I'm her boss, remember? There are lines I can't cross."

Casey snorts. "From what you've told me, it sounds like you crossed plenty of lines already. And that Sophie enjoyed crossing them with you. You haven't told me *why* she wanted you to leave her alone. Care to share?"

"Not really."

"Yes, you do." Casey's teasing words are accompanied by a series of pokes to the ribs. Why do older sisters always know the exact spot to tickle you to get their way?

"She wanted to date in secret, I wanted to date her for real. Every time I tried to do something nice for her, she would refuse it. Say it was too much."

Casey is silent next to me, letting me talk. Knowing she'll understand what I mean without me having to explain or hedge my thoughts, it all comes out in a rush.

"Case, she said that sending her a forty-dollar fruit arrangement was *too expensive*. That it was buying her affection and made her feel like a hooker. A hooker? You have no idea how smart and kind she is. I was *proud* to have her on my arm at the Youth in Tech event. God dammit, Case, I walked around that event thinking I was the luckiest man in the room to have such an amazing woman with me. Why can't she see that?"

Pausing to take a breath, I risk a glance at my phone to avoid looking at Casey. Nothing. "She's so worried about Emma's hospital bill—but I would have paid it in an instant, if she would just ask. Instead, she applied to the company employee emergency fund. Did you know she and Emma share a one-bedroom apartment? Sophie sleeps on the couch so her daughter can have the bedroom. Every night I lay in my big, expensive bed, in my giant house, and I die inside thinking about her curled up on that sad old couch. I could buy her a house, or a new car, and not even notice the difference to my bank statement. But she insists on staying a secret. And she won't ask for help, even though I know she needs it."

We're silent for a moment, while I attempt to collect my thoughts and calm my racing heart. The silence is broken by Casey's quiet voice of reason beside me. "Trust me when I say, you can't force someone to take your help if they don't want it, Teddy. Even when you're watching them hurt themselves. And it kills you with each breath, terrified it could be their last." I wince at the reminder of her and Garrett's past, the years they each spent in and out of rehab before they found their happily ever after together. "It seems so simple to us, to throw money at the problem. But it can't be easy to accept when your pride is the only thing you have enough of."

She lets me stew on her words for a second as a squawk from the baby monitor has her half off the couch, ready to go see what's wrong with Clara. When no more noise follows, she sighs and curls back into my side. I wrap one arm around her shoulder, finding comfort in the warmth and weight of her against me. "I do understand Sophie's need to not go public with you. You forget, little brother, most people didn't grow up on red carpets and dealing with the paparazzi on a daily basis. She's not as tough as you and has way more to lose."

"That's what Mercedes said. I'm starting to think you might be right."

"Mercedes said it? Yes!" She pumps a fist in the air. "If Mercedes agrees then you know I'm right. So, what did Mercedes say you should do?"

"She told me to stop cornering Sophie and let her take the lead."

Casey nods. "I agree."

"But how can I let her take the lead when she won't even talk to me? She hasn't been at work all week and she hasn't reached out once." I scrub my free hand over my face, pulling on my chin. I haven't been shaving like usual, my normal light beard grown out and shaggy. I tug at it, my skin itchy with the California heat.

"Have you reached out to make sure she's okay? Not with an agenda, but just to check in. Don't offer any help, just let her know you're thinking of her. If she wants to respond she will."

"And if she doesn't?"

"Then maybe, little bro, you really have to let her go."

Twenty-three

SOPHIE

Tall, Dark and Handsome: I don't know if this is crossing a line, but I'm worried about you. You don't have to explain anything, but please let me know if you're ok.

I'VE READ TEDDY'S TEXT a hundred times in the last hour, my internal debate shifting from *if* I should respond, to *how* I should respond. My instinct is to answer right away and reassure him that I'm fine. To tell him a partial truth, that I'm taking the PTO I never use to be with Emma, leaving out the part that I know will hurt him.

But doing that feels entirely too comfortable. Like an old threadbare t-shirt that I've worn a thousand times, because that's exactly how I used to be with Jake. Tell him only the things that won't upset him, let him think that everything is fine, even when I'm dying inside.

That feeling may be comfortable, but I'm beginning to suspect it's so worn it's going to disintegrate.

My fingers hover over the keyboard on my phone, typing and deleting the message a dozen times without sending any of them.

I'm taking some time to be with Emma.

The truth, but not the whole truth.

I appreciate your concern. I'm fine, just taking care of some things.

He deserves better than a half-formal brush-off.

I'm okay. Emma is okay. I just needed a break.

That's closer to the truth—I do need a break. But I need a break as in some good luck, not as in time off from work.

In the end, Emma gives me the answer when I quiz her for the thousandth time before letting her leave to spend the night at Bella's.

"Mom, stop, I'm fine. You're the one who looks like they're going to collapse from exhaustion. Go take a nap or something." She and Bella giggle at my scowl before Emma leans in to kiss my cheek. "I'm kidding. Sort of. You really should take a nap, though. Or you know, whatever you feel like doing. But not cleaning."

I swat her butt as she slips away, before collapsing on the couch, phone in hand. Typing out the truth before I can chicken out, I toss my phone on the coffee table and grab my laptop, clicking open the browser I left full of job search results.

> **Me:** *Thank you for checking on me. I'm fine, Emma's fine. Taking some time to try and build a more sustainable future for us both. One that doesn't leave me short on sleep and long on stress.*

I click open and apply for two more copywriting positions before I allow myself to check for a response. I know perfectly well there isn't one since my phone hasn't made a sound, but I have to check anyway.

What I can't resist, is knowing if he's as broken-hearted as I am.

Unlocking it, I'm rewarded with the sight of those three little dots. They appear and disappear over and over. Either he's writing an essay or he's started his reply over more times than me. Why doesn't that make me feel any better?

> **Tall, Dark and Handsome:** *If there's anything I can do to help, please tell me, Sunshine.*

Sunshine. Seeing it there, that he still thinks of me that way, has regret flooding my chest. To keep the tears at bay, I make myself look around my apartment. The walls and once-white appliances in the kitchen are slightly yellowed with age and the dust I can never get rid of. This pull-out couch that I bought off Craigslist is exactly as comfortable as the fifty bucks I paid for it would suggest. A spring pokes into my ass as I shift.

It's not that our home is dirty—Emma and I cleaned and tidied up this morning—it's just that it's old and faded and crowded with the stuff we've accumulated over the years. It fit better in the three-bedroom house we used to rent. But that's just one more casualty of scraping by for all those years. No matter how many times we said we were going to save up for a down payment to try and buy a house one day, there was always some reason why the money disappeared before it could make it to our savings account.

Instead of letting my mind wander down that well-worn path of regret, I type out a response and go back to my job hunting.

> **Me:** *I appreciate the offer, but I don't think there's anything you can do.*

I apply to a dozen more jobs, ear tuned for the buzz of an incoming text, but it never comes. Instead of letting myself dwell on the disappointment curled up in my belly, I open up a blank document and start writing. Anything is better than this hollowness inside my chest.

An hour later I've got three hundred or so words each on stories about a dog going missing, a daughter dealing with her mother's Alzheimer's diagnosis, and a magical princess who's about to be married off to the most pathetic knight in her father's kingdom.

Writing has always been how I dealt with my issues. Mad at Jake? Write him as the villain in my next story. Bored at work? Write a fantastical fantasy adventure. Sitting alone in a hospital room while my husband is God knows where? Write a sexy island romance and pretend I'm living it.

Lauren is the only person who's ever read any of my fiction though. Nothing I write is important enough to spend what little energy I have in attempting to publish it. I publish enough under Elinor Price's name, and I don't have the resources or the time to pursue either traditional or self-publishing.

Trading my laptop for my phone, I nearly drop it when a text pops up.

> **Tall, Dark and Handsome:** *There's probably a lot of things I could do to help, but since you don't seem to want my assistance, I won't push.*

> **Me:** *I appreciate that, but you don't owe me anything. I don't want you to feel obligated.*

> **Tall, Dark and Handsome:** *I don't feel obligated. I WANT to help. I care about you, Sunshine. When you care about someone, you want to lighten their load. I just want you to know that when, or if, you ever need it, the answer will always be yes.*

He cares about me? I know I care about him, more than I want to admit, but I never thought I was anything more than a distraction to him.

His words to me in Seattle come floating back up to the surface of my mind. *Anything, everything. It's all yours, Sunshine.* The glimpse I'd had of his face when he said it, the vulnerability, the hope sparkling in his eyes before he'd buried his face into my neck. He means it, and he's the one who's been brave enough to say it out loud, unlike me.

But still, the idea of asking for his help grates a nerve inside me that I can't ignore. I don't want to be rescued. I want to rescue myself.

> **Me:** *Thank you. Where are you? You haven't been to the office?*

> **Tall, Dark and Handsome:** *I'm in CA visiting Casey and the kids. I thought you were taking the week off?*

> **Me:** *I came back on Thursday. Tina requested the days off months ago. How's the family? Happy to see you?*

I can almost hear his growl in response to my shallow questions.

> **Tall, Dark and Handsome:** *Are you home alone right now?*

> **Me:** *Yes. Why?*

Instead of a text, my phone vibrates with an incoming video call. I am not prepared for a video call. My hair is greasy and twisted up on my head, I'm not wearing any makeup and the angry red zit on my chin is on full display. Not to mention I'm wearing an old ratty sweatshirt with stains on it, and an old pair of Jake's boxers that I refuse to give up.

I hit decline and throw my phone across the couch, where it immediately buzzes.

Tall, Dark and Handsome: *Answer the phone Sunshine.*

Me: *I am not video calling you, I look disgusting right now.*

Tall, Dark and Handsome: *I don't care, I just want to see your face.*

Me: *Nope, not going to happen.*

My heart slows to a less frantic pace as I take back control of the conversation. I don't have to see his stupidly handsome face if I don't want to.

Tall, Dark and Handsome: *Sunshine. Answer the damn phone.*

I could draw this out, turn it into a flirtatious fight. But as fun as that would be, I'm too tired of fighting Theo to enjoy it. I won't win against the stubborn bastard and he knows it. So I do the smarter thing instead.

"I don't want to fight over it. No video." I say the second he picks up.

His growly sigh has goosebumps prickling down my spine. "Sunshine. Why are you such a pain in my ass?"

"Only to you. Everyone else thinks I'm made of lollipops and cotton candy. I'm a fucking joy." The teasing words are out before I can stop myself. Theo's chuckle tickling my ear is intoxicating, making me want to keep going, even though the flirty banter is dangerous territory.

He interrupts me before I can get going though. "Sophie-fucking joy-Alexander. What am I going to do with you?"

"I don't know, sir. You're the one who was trying to call me. What do you need?"

There's a long silence before he answers. "I need a lot of things. I called because I didn't want to type out a long response to your question. Casey and the kids are good. Missing Garrett, but otherwise good."

"That's good. I'm glad you got to see them. I'm sure you miss your family."

"I do. But I think coming here may have been a mistake."

My heart stops.

"A mistake? Why do you think that?"

There's another long sigh in my ear. God, I miss his growly voice. The rumble of it does things to my newly awake lady bits and I have to rub my thighs together to ease some of the heat building in my core.

"Seeing the way my sister misses Garrett just makes me miss you more." Theo's confession is a dagger to my heart. He misses me? What on earth can I possibly offer him to miss? He pauses when I don't answer. "Sunshine? What are you doing? What's that noise?"

I bite my lips for a second, fighting back tears. "Nothing. I'm fine."

"Are you crying?"

"No." I lie.

"Sunshine..." When I don't answer he sighs into the phone. "Are you sure there's nothing I can do to help you out with whatever it is you're doing?"

And just like that, my tears dry up. I have to do this on my own. "Theo, stop. I need to do this myself. For me. I need to know that I can. I'm sorry if it's not what you want, but it's what I need to do."

My phone buzzes against my ear, I pull back to see an email notification. Not just any email—the one I've been waiting for.

"I have to go. Thank you for checking on me. I hope you enjoy the rest of your trip." I hate how impersonal I sound, but if I don't get off the phone with Theo in the next ten seconds all my secrets are going to explode out of me.

"Oh. Um. Okay. I guess I'll let you go." He sounds so confused at my abrupt change that guilt floods my gut. "I'll see you at the office on Monday, right?"

"Yes. Goodnight, Teddy."

"Goodnight, Sunshine."

The guilt sits in my belly like a brick as I open the email. It only gets worse as I read the good news.

I thought this was going to be the answer to all my problems, so why does it feel like I'm doing the wrong thing for all the right reasons?

"Well. I don't think any of us saw that coming." The head of Mailbox's HR department straightens her glasses. "But, I do understand your situation. A lot of people here are going to be sorry to see you go."

I have to clear my throat twice before I can speak, the tears I've been fighting back all day threatening. I couldn't make eye contact with Theo when he stalked through the lobby this morning.

Especially when he slowed down as he passed my desk, mouth opening as if to speak. Thank God the phone rang right then, and by the time I was finished the elevator doors were already closing on his perfect face.

"I'm going to miss this place too, Kate. But I need to do what's best for me and my daughter." Giving my two-week's notice at Mailbox is the scariest thing I've ever done. Even scarier than the job interviews I went on last week while I was taking my time off.

Kate leans back to read something on her screen. "Are you going to continue as one of our freelance contributors as Elinor Price? That is a separate contract from your regular employment contract."

"Oh. Can I do that?"

"It may depend on if your new job has you sign any kind of non-compete clause with them. Do you want to hold off on making a decision until you have more details?"

"That would be great." I twist the hem of my cardigan through my fingers, nerves hitting me all at once. Am I really doing this? Leaving the safety of Mailbox to venture out on my own?

Fear and pride fight for space in my chest. The non-profit I worked for before coming to Mailbox had hired me straight out of college, but that was after years of me volunteering with them. And even though I'd had to apply and interview at Mailbox like anyone else, knowing that Lauren was here and probably putting in a good word for me, made it feel like we'd accomplished it together, not that I'd gotten the job on my own.

Lauren.

She's going to kill me when she finds out I'm leaving. I should have told her last night, but she'd come over after another disaster of a date and I hadn't wanted to make her feel any worse.

"There are just a few details to iron out with the Employee Relief Fund application you put in two weeks ago."

"I'm sorry, what?"

"Your application was approved two weeks ago, but the payment hasn't been processed."

What is she talking about? "My application?"

Kate stops clicking through screens to look at me. "Your application to the Employee Relief Fund? You don't remember? You filed it on..." She clicks a few times then reads me the day after Emma's surgery. "Mr. Sutton approved it himself right away, but usually the funds go on your next paycheck, which isn't for another few days. I'll just need to get an approval from him to include it on your final paycheck."

Panic pushes my confusion aside. "Wait!" Kate freezes, staring at me around the corner of her monitor. "Um. I don't need it anymore. You can cancel the application."

"For thirty-thousand dollars?" Her face softening, Kate keeps talking while my mind races. "I don't want to overstep, Sophie, but surely you could use the help? You've been paying into the fund since you started here years ago. Just because you're leaving doesn't mean you don't have the right to utilize it now that you need it. This is exactly what it's for."

"I just feel guilty for taking it when I'm not going to be an employee here any longer. Besides, I wasn't the one who submitted it. And thirty-thousand dollars is way too much. I thought the limit was ten?" My confusion comes roaring back. Did Theo do this behind my back? Find a way to sneak me the money when he knew I wouldn't take it directly from him?

"Hmmm, you're right. Hang on." Kate is silent, reading the notes on her screen. "It looks like the original application was for fifteen-thousand, which is the normal limit," Kate adds, looking up. "But a second application was made within the system to double the amount."

"But...you can't do that?" I don't understand what's happening. I'd started filling out the application under Lauren's watchful eye at the hospital the moment we found out that Jake didn't have his health insurance, or the job that went with it, anymore. But I never completed it, too embarrassed for Theo to know how in need of it I was.

Kate cuts me off before I can say any more. "Enough of that. You've more than earned the right to that assistance and it was all approved by Mr. Sutton himself. Whether it's against the rules or not, he made the decision to approve all thirty-thousand, no strings attached. Someone obviously knows you well enough to know not only that you needed it, but that you deserved a helping hand. Maybe you should find that person and thank them. Besides," she steam-rolls my objection, "it's already done. We're just waiting on the check to be signed."

I swallow my argument. I can't tell her that the man who signs the check is the exact reason I'm worried.

Twenty-four

THEO

I SHOULD HAVE STAYED in California. Then I wouldn't be tempted to march downstairs and haul Sophie up to my office to explain to me what the hell she's playing at.

The email from HR stares back at me from my monitor, my approval to release the relief funds on her final check the only reason I was notified of her resignation. Under normal circumstances, I wouldn't have known until I walked in one day to be greeted by a new face.

Pushing back from my desk, I pace the length of my office. Anger that she's leaving, and didn't even have the decency to tell me first, competes with the black hole opening in my chest. The one that reminds me over and over that I'm not going to see her face every morning when I walk in, that I won't see her smile every evening when I leave.

I didn't know how much I needed it until now.

"Sir?" Mercedes' question stops me in my tracks, hands buried in my hair, a growl dying in my throat at the sight of her pitying expression. "Mr. Edwards is here." When I don't respond she steps into my space, closing the door behind her. "Sir? Are you okay?"

"Does it look like I'm okay?" I snap.

Mercedes eyes me like one of her unruly grandkids. Fuck. I should apologize, but she speaks before I can say anything. "I assume this has something to do with the email from HR?"

At my nod, her face softens. "I can take care of it for you while you meet with Mr. Edwards."

"No. Thank you." I bite out the words. "I'll take care of it after he leaves. I just..." I can't hold onto the anger any longer, the heat dissipating from my chest with a defeated sigh as sadness takes its place. "Send him in."

Mercedes gives me another moment to pull my game face on. I tuck my hurt feelings aside and pull on the stern facade of Theodore just in time. The moment Mercedes opens the door, Morgan pushes past her to step into my office.

"How was California? I see you managed to avoid the paps." Unbuttoning his jacket, Morgan doesn't wait for me before lounging in one of the chairs at my desk.

I slide into my own leather chair, the open window on my screen reminding me of Sophie's betrayal. I minimize it before answering Morgan, reminding myself who I'm dealing with and not to let Sophie's name pass my lips. "Why would I need to avoid the paparazzi? I was at my sister's house the whole time."

"I assumed some up-and-coming starlet was in need of your attention when you went down there so suddenly." He chuckles at his own joke and I suppress my shudder. Morgan Edwards is my mentor in a lot of things, but his attitude about women is not one of them.

"The only up-and-coming starlet I saw was my niece, Clara. She has a winning smile, but isn't very good at learning her lines yet."

"Hmph. Never mind that. What new and exciting project do you have for me?"

I spend the next hour outlining the groundwork we'd laid out on the new project, the embedded video editing software to go with the medical record manager I started developing. Once we get past the comparison to social media apps, Morgan is all business, pointing out issues and pitfalls as we go. We keep talking until Mercedes shoos us out of the building to get lunch.

"I see you kept the pretty one." Morgan points out as we pass Tina alone at the front desk.

"What do you mean, the pretty one?" The growl in my voice should be a warning, but Morgan doesn't hear it.

"Oh, don't give me that. I know perfectly well you'd never dip your pen in the company ink—I taught you better than that—but there's no harm in looking. And appreciating." His chuckle grates against every nerve in my body. If only he knew exactly how deep I dipped my...pen. The image of Sophie spread out in my bed, her blond locks cascading over the pillow, her sunshine smile lighting up my home, her giggle vibrating against my soul, flashes in my mind. I can hardly breathe from the need to hold her again.

"Although I might make an exception for that content director of yours, what's her name? Masterson? She looks like she knows the art of a well-placed—"

"Morgan, that's enough." My warning is interrupted by a series of texts from the dev team on the new project. "I have to go put out some fires. I'll have Mercedes loop you in on the project." I try not to let my relief show at avoiding further conversation as I head back into the building.

The new developer, the one I yelled at unnecessarily, is waiting for me in the lobby. "What is it, Frankie?" I remind myself to be nice—she hasn't done anything wrong.

"S-s-sir, the team sent me to meet you down here." She stutters and doesn't make eye contact, her fingers twisting in the hem of her shirt.

Are those fuckwits trying to haze her? "They sent you to meet me in the lobby? Did they not get the message that I was on my way?"

"They d-did." Her eyes dart around, but there's no one here except us and Julian. "Is something wrong?"

I rub my forehead, a headache already forming. "Those assholes are trying to get you in trouble." I head toward the elevator bank, resolutely not looking at Sophie's empty desk as I pass it. "Julian?" I call, shaking my head.

"On it, sir." He reaches over to push the call button, Frankie trailing behind me.

We wait in silence for the doors to open, the only sound an occasional sniff from behind my left shoulder. Finally, the doors open and I step inside, my hands shoved deep in my pockets.

"I'll send her right up after you." Julian nods as he places a restraining hand on Frankie's shoulder, stopping her from following me.

She looks at him, then at me, confusion written on her face. "But—"

"Mr. Sutton doesn't—"

The ridiculousness of my rule never to share the elevator hits me like a ton of bricks. I slap a hand to the edge of the door, holding it open. "It's fine. Come on Ms. Emory. Let's go see what the problem is."

"It's okay, I can take the stairs." Her voice is so quiet I can hardly hear it.

"Don't be ridiculous, we're going to the tenth floor." My tone is sharper than I intended so I do my best to soften my expression. The way Sophie teased me about it, about being unable to stop glaring, when we were in Seattle twists my stomach. "Come, Ms. Emory."

Timidly, she steps inside and we ride up to the tenth floor in silence, apart from her sniffing.

The rest of my day is packed. Once I sufficiently growl the dev team into leaving Frankie alone, we get to work solving the issue they'd run into. The never-ending day ends with a marketing and sales team meeting. None of it does anything to improve my mood, especially once I carve out the two minutes needed to approve the distribution of funds for Sophie's final check.

My anger at Sophie's betrayal bursts out of me at the slightest provocation all day, earning one of the guys from sales a dressing down that was possibly harsher than called for. But anyone who is stupid enough to offer up his date to an art gallery opening in exchange for a colleague's fancy paper shredder doesn't deserve to have a woman on his arm at any type of function.

Not even seeing Ms. Masterson try to hide her grin at Stuart's humble apology makes me feel better. I cut the meeting short just after six and send everyone home before I fire someone just for the pleasure of it. For a split second, I think that Ms. Masterson is going to stay and ask me a question, but after staring at me for a long moment, she follows everyone else out of the room.

The emotional roller-coaster I've been on all day has me wrung out. My anger at Sophie and the dev team assholes, the realization that I've been needlessly selfish about my privacy at the office, weighs me down as I walk out the doors for the night.

As I turn onto my street, most of my anger has been replaced by sadness. It's really truly over. Sophie doesn't want anything to do with me. If she did, why would she be leaving Mailbox?

I jerk to a stop in my driveway at the sight of Emma sitting on the front steps, one arm wrapped around her knees as she scrolls through her phone. What the hell is she doing here? Is Sophie okay? Worry and confusion fight in my chest as I climb out of my car.

"Emma? What are you doing here? Is your mom okay?"

She scrambles to her feet, blond hair so achingly familiar to Sophie's flying in her face. "Hi. Oof." She stops for a second with her hand on her stomach.

I start forward but she waves me away. "I'm fine, it's just a twinge from standing up so fast."

"How did you get here? Shouldn't you be home recovering?" I don't know a lot about kids and appendix surgery, but I'm pretty sure that Emma shouldn't be walking two miles to my house two weeks post-op.

"It's fine, I'm fine. It doesn't hurt, it just feels kind of weird every once in a while. And I walked, which is what I wanted to talk to you about." The cautious smile she gives me is hard to resist, it's so similar to Sophie's.

There's a thud at the door before Max's barking can be heard. "I'm coming, I'm coming," I call, stepping past Emma to open the front door. "We better go inside before he breaks the door down." I open it and step back to let her through. Emma rushes past me, immediately squatting down in front of Max, scratching his ears and talking to him.

I leave them in the open door to put my work bag and jacket down on the dining room table. I should shut the front door, but I'm nervous to close myself in the house with Sophie's fifteen-year-old daughter, especially since I have no idea what she wants or why she's here.

Instead, I grab Max's longest leash and clip it on him between pets from Emma. "Okay, let's take him out front and you can tell me what's going on and why you're here." I don't mean to be gruff with her, but something in my tone must give her a warning that I'm not in the mood to be nice, because she straightens up immediately and grabs his leash.

"I got him. Come on, Max."

I follow her out the door and sit on the stoop, letting her take Max out onto the grass in front. She watches him for a second before turning to me with a big inhale, like she's practiced whatever it is she's about to say. I brace myself for whatever is about to come, sending up an internal prayer to whoever is listening that she doesn't put me in an untenable situation.

"Right, okay. So here's the thing." Her voice is steady, but the way her fingers twist the leash in her hand gives away her nerves. "I need money."

I can't stop the twist in my face at her words any more than I can stop the disappointment that settles in my gut. Of course. How could I expect anything less? I push back up to my feet, but she stops me with her next words. "Wait! I didn't say that right. I need to *earn* money."

"Why?" The word is more of a growl, but I'm beyond being nice right now.

Emma looks away, her eyes darting to Max and back to me. "Um. I just do."

"Emma..."

Max sniffs the bush at the end of my yard, interested in whatever dog left his calling card there earlier. If I focus on him, maybe I won't yell at the reminder of who I lost, staring at me from the middle of my yard.

"It's not for anything bad, I promise, Teddy. I just..." Some of her hair falls in her face and she blows it away, her face transforming from a young lady negotiating her first business deal to a little kid in that second. It reminds me of baby Clara, laughing and blowing bubbles in her food. My heart twitches in my chest at the sight. How does this kid get under my skin so easily? It's unfair.

I deflate at the uncertainty in her face. Emma hasn't done anything. I can't growl and intimidate her into saying what I want to hear, it would be wrong and I know it. "So you need to earn money and can't tell me why. What is your proposal?"

"Let me walk Max for you a couple times a week."

"No." The pain in my chest at turning Emma down is sharp and hard. If only she knew how desperately I wish I could say yes, to keep that tie to both her and Sophie

Emma's eyes go wide at my sharp word. "But, don't you have to work late sometimes?"

"No."

"But—"

"No."

Max comes bounding over, oblivious to the standoff between us. He licks Emma's leg in passing before plopping down in front of me. Emma crosses her arms, one teenage hip cocked to the side. It takes everything in me not to smile at the expression on her face, one that Sophie has given me more than once.

"Why not?"

"Because it's not appropriate, Emma."

"Bullshit. How else am I supposed to earn some money? There are no kids in our apartment complex for me to babysit. Babysitting and dog-walking are my only marketable skills." She shrugs. "And don't say it's because my mom works for you," she adds before I can open my mouth.

"Not anymore." The words are out of my mouth before I can stop myself. It's only as the shock registers across Emma's face that I realize my mistake.

"What?" Her shriek is loud enough to send Max scrambling behind me. "Did you *fire* my mom?"

Leaping to my feet, I fumble with Max's leash and my own hands, not sure what to do with them in the face of an upset and outraged teenage girl. "No wait, I'm sorry, that wasn't what I—"

"Did you fire my mom? Why? Is it because of me? Because she took all that time off to be with me?"

"No, I promise that's not what—" I stop to take a breath and think about how to diffuse the situation. "Emma, listen to me for a second. I didn't fire Sophie, I promise. She put in her notice today. Didn't you know? She hasn't been at work all afternoon, I assumed she was home with you."

The questions and vague rumblings coming from Emma stop. "What? No. I mean, no I didn't know. She quit? Why would she quit? Okay, well now you really have to let me walk Max for you 'cause if she—"

It's my turn to interrupt, try to get the conversation back to safe ground. "Hang on, just take a second. Let's start this whole thing over. You want me to pay you to walk Max a couple days a week because you need money. Why do you need the money, Emma?"

Cheeks pink, Emma takes a comically deep breath before blurting out, "Well, originally I wanted to earn the money 'cause I know that the bill from my hospital stay was stupid big, because my stupid dad didn't tell my mom that his insurance got cancelled because he lost his job *again,* so I wanted to help with the bill maybe a little, or at least not have to ask her for money for stuff. But if she quit her job then we *really* need the money so please, please, Teddy let me walk Max. Please?"

I don't know if it's the extra 'please' at the end or the panicked tears spilling down Emma's cheeks that rip the last Band-aid holding my heart together, but the anger and blackness that have been threatening me ever since I saw that email crash over me. A tidal wave of emotion I can't control or outsmart engulfs me. I don't even bother to fight it anymore—I'm too tired of fighting it. So I do the one thing I shouldn't. I open my big mouth.

"What the actual fuck is happening right now? I said no, Emma, and I meant it. If your mom wants my help she's going to have to grow a pair and ask me for it herself. Not apply for the company fund or ask her kid to walk my fucking dog. I can't fucking believe this. This is a joke right?" I pace up and down the lawn in front of my house. "First, your mom gets under my skin with her daily 'Good Morning, Mr. Sutton' routine, and somehow I come to count on it to start my day. Then she shows up for the gala as Elinor and is so goddamn sexy and full of sass and it completely takes me by surprise. And we have the most amazing time together, but does she want to date me? No, she wants to keep it a secret. Will she let me take her out? I have to practically kidnap her to get her to go on a fucking *date*. And God forbid I offer to help in any way."

I glare at Emma, as if she has any control over the situation. I should stop talking, she doesn't want to hear this, but the words pour out of me.

"Oh no. Not Sophie, she can't accept any help when it's offered. She'll just slave away and work for pennies when I'm offering her everything. Jesus fucking Christ, she's driving me crazy. And then to top it all off, she'll accept help from strangers, from anyone but *me*. Why not me, huh, Emma?"

The last word is more of a gasp than anything as I drag oxygen into my lungs. Emma's eyes are wide as saucers at my verbal vomit. "Fuck. I shouldn't have said any of that to you. God dammit. I can't—" I suck in a breath as the magnitude of what I've said to Emma dawns on me. "Can you...I should take you home. Is that okay? Am I allowed to drive you home?"

"Um, why wouldn't you be allowed to drive me home? Also, you and my mom dated?"

"That's what you got out of that? Yes, Emma. Well, I tried to date your mom, but she made it very difficult. I managed to take her out a grand total of two times before she—never mind." I sigh. "Stay here, I'll be right back."

I hand her Max's leash and dash into the house to grab my car keys and collect my thoughts. Once inside the safety of my home, I let loose a string of expletives as I pace to my dining room table. What the hell is going on?

First Sophie quits without so much as a heads up. Was she that afraid of my reaction? Is she so unwilling to see me that she had to leave Mailbox? Did I really screw things up so badly? All I did was offer to help, I don't understand why it feels like Sophie would rather see or talk to anyone but me. After our conversation the other night I thought I had a chance again. Then today the rug's been pulled out from under me.

Now Emma is here, asking for a job walking Max. I want to help the kid out—I get that feeling of not wanting to be a burden. God, I used to hate it when my mom would give me "spending money" that I knew had come from Casey's last paycheck. But how can I let her walk Max when Sophie doesn't want anything to do with me? Wouldn't that be betraying Sophie?

My fingers trace the outline of my phone in my pocket. I could text Sophie and ask her what she wants me to do. But I'm so angry at her I don't think I can be civil. Better to just take Emma home and avoid the subject. If Sophie wants to slink away without a word, I'll let her.

Maybe.

I swipe my keys from my coat pocket and storm back out the door, locking it behind me. "Let's go."

Emma looks up from her spot sitting in the grass, Max draped over her legs, his belly offered up for the scratches she's doling out. "Go?"

"Hop in the car, I'll take you home."

I lean down to swipe the end of Max's leash. "Come on, traitor." I tug and Max rolls to his feet. "You can come too."

Emma doesn't speak until we're all in the car, Max drooling out the window. "Let me get this straight. You took my mom out on a couple of dates, but now she won't talk to you. And you're mad she quit Mailbox, but you won't let me walk Max because you think my mom told me to do it? That makes no sense." She pauses, as if waiting for me to answer, but I stay silent. "So....You really like my mom, huh?"

The sneak attack catches me off guard, but I manage to clamp down and only grunt in response.

"Oh, okay Witcher. If that's how you want to play it."

"Emma," I growl in response. "Drop it."

She hums, reaching back to scratch Max's ears as I turn onto her street. "No, I don't think I will. You don't scare me, mister."

"I should."

"Why? Because you might fire my mom? She already quit."

The direct hit to my ego stings, making my next words sharp. "I thought you wanted a job walking Max?"

"I do, but if you say no, there's nothing I can do. But if you like my mom..."

She pauses and I glance away from the road to see her twisting her head from side to side, like she's debating with herself. "Out with it. If I like your mom...what?"

"If you and my mom are dating, wouldn't I get to walk Max anyways?"

"Your mom doesn't want to date me." Thank God their shitty apartment complex is in view, I don't know how much more I can take. I pull in and stop the car just in front of their building.

"But if she did..."

The incessant questions snap something inside me and I lash out. "But she doesn't, Emma. Your mom didn't want to be seen with me in public, did she? She'd rather be my fucking side-piece than have anyone know she was with me. I don't think your mom has any idea how amazing she is, and she deserves to be with someone who's going to remind her of it and treat her like the cardigan-wearing badass she is. Your dad—sorry, kid—he's fucking trash, and I never want her to feel like she did because of him again. It kills me to see her still struggling because of the choices he's made. Especially when I could easily make it all go away."

"My dad is a waste of oxygen—I've known it for years." Emma sighs, thumping her head against the seat. "How did you know Elinor was my mom?"

"How could I not?" I grind out, barely keeping my volume in check. "I see her every day. When she showed up as Elinor I thought it was a joke, but then I saw a new side of Sophie that night. And I liked it. A lot. But the evening was a disaster, or so I thought. Then she texted and—"

The kid does not need to know about the weekend we spent secluded in my bed so I cut myself off.

"And when I finally managed to get your mom to come out with me, it ended with you in the emergency room and she cut me off again. I can't keep up anymore."

I sigh and flop back against my seat, waiting for the unusually subdued Emma to climb out of the car. But she doesn't even undo her seatbelt, she just stares at me. "What?"

She doesn't flinch at my bark. "I changed my mind. I don't want you to hire me to walk Max."

"Fine. I'm glad we agree. Now get out before someone calls the cops on me."

"Nope." She crosses her arms and leans against her door, daring me to say something with a quirk of her eyebrow. If only she knew how much she looks like her mom when she does that. And how much it hurts. "You need my help."

"No, I don't. Goodbye, Emma." I hit the button to unlock the door but no way am I reaching across her to pop the door open. She doesn't move.

Leaning back against my own door I mirror her pose. If she thinks she can out-stubborn me, she's in for a surprise. Smug, I cross my arms and raise my own eyebrow. It's a practiced look that has brought more than one business rival to his knees.

Emma doesn't even flinch.

"Is that supposed to scare me?" Her smart mouth takes me by surprise and I barely hold onto my scowl. "Listen Teddy—I'm gonna call you Teddy no matter how deeply you furrow those eyebrows at me. You need me. You need me more than I need you, I bet. I just wanted to earn a couple of bucks walking your dog, but now I find out that you want something much more valuable."

I cock my head, curious where she's going with this, but absolutely certain that this fifteen-year-old terrorist has me by the balls and knows it. "And what's that?"

"Well, the way I see it, we both want the same thing. I want my mom to be less stressed-out all the time. She's always worried about something—me, money, Max, Lauren, my stupid dad. You know who she never worries about? Herself."

I can't help the snort that escapes me. Emma grins before schooling her face again, the negotiator back in charge.

"*You* want my mom. To date or whatever."

"Not whatever." I need to make sure Emma understands I'm in this for real, not on a whim. She may be playing at being a grownup at the moment, but I'm not. "I want to date your mom, period. She deserves someone who's going to take care of her, make her life easier, better. I want to be that for her."

"Right." She nods, her blond hair bouncing around with the force. "Listen." She leans forward, digging a finger into my shoulder. "If I didn't believe you, we wouldn't be having this conversation. I could make your life miserable if I wanted to." She leans back, hands up. "I like you—for now—so I won't. But I could. Don't forget that."

Shaking my head, I run a hand over my chin to hide the smile threatening to make an appearance. Mid-negotiation is not the time. "Do you have an actual proposal or just threats?"

Twenty-five

SOPHIE

Max glares at me with his good eye as I let myself into Lauren's apartment. He doesn't move from his sunny spot on the couch, but his tail waves lazily a few times before he goes back to sleep.

"Hey, Maxy." My voice is loud in the quiet of her apartment, despite my almost whisper. Lauren won't be home for another hour or so, she was in a meeting when I left and traffic was a bitch getting here. I glance around her kitchen as I set my purse on the floor. She's obviously been working later nights than I thought, based on the dirty dishes in the sink and the empty wine bottle on the counter.

With nothing better to do while I wait, I empty the dishwasher and reload it. The recycling is too full to add the bottle, but rather than sit here on my phone, I pull the bag out to take it to the dumpster.

Locking the front door behind me, I grip the bag and take off down the stairs.

"You're not Lauren." The accusation has me whirling back to face it, halfway down the cement steps. An old man is standing half out of the doorway opposite Lauren's, glaring at me.

"No, I'm not." I cut myself off from asking any more questions. He must be in his eighties, the bald top of his head ringed by wispy white hair like a priest. "She's my friend, I was just taking out the trash for her." I half lift the bag in my hand to prove it.

"Hmph. So that was you making all that noise earlier?" Ok-ay, so the wrinkles are more of the 'get off my lawn' variety than the 'did I ever tell you about the time' variety. "You tell Lauren I don't appreciate her friends coming over and making a racket in the middle of the day."

Who the hell is this guy? He definitely didn't live here when Emma and I were staying with Lauren last year. Has it really been that long since I've come over?

"I didn't mean to disturb you, sir."

He harrumphs at my apology and slams his door shut before I can say anything else. I'll have to ask Lauren about her new neighbor.

Forty-five minutes later, I'm adding some frozen peas to my impromptu stir fry when Lauren walks in the door. "Soph? What are you doing here? And does it have anything to do with why Sutton was in the foulest mood I've ever seen?"

She drops her bag on the floor and scoops up Max who's been wandering around underfoot waiting for me to drop another piece of kung pao chicken. "That smells delicious. How did you find anything to cook? I haven't gone grocery shopping in weeks."

"The leftover Chinese in your fridge smelled okay, so I just cooked some new rice to go with it." I point to the rice cooker on her countertop, white steam bubbling away in it. "Also, I'm mad at you."

"Mad at me? What did I do?" She reaches over my shoulder to pluck a piece of chicken from the pan and pop it in her mouth. "Why are you cooking for me if you're mad at me?"

"Because I was hungry."

"But why are you mad?" She snatches another bite of chicken and I smack her hand with the wooden spoon in mine. "You're being very nice to me?"

"I am nice."

"You're an asshole with a smile and we both know it, Soph. What's up?"

I pull plates down from her cupboard and start dividing up the food. "I'm mad at you and Sutton equally. *You* went behind my back to apply for the assistance fund, after I told you I didn't want you to."

Lauren heaps her plate with rice, chicken and the vegetables I'd found in the back of her freezer. "Soph..." she groans. "You need the money. And you've been paying into that program since you started. That's what it's fucking *for*. Medical emergencies are, like, the first thing on the list of reasons why you can apply. Besides, all I did was finish the application you started. You can't really be mad at me?"

I fill my own plate while she perches on one of the stools at her counter. Her dining room table is piled high with packages from various clothing stores. "That's what Kate said too." Leaning my elbows on the counter opposite her, I shovel a forkful of dinner into my mouth. "Hot!"

Her grin is evil as I chew carefully, trying not to burn the inside of my mouth any more. "HR Kate?" I don't answer and she eyes me. "So why are you mad at Sutton? Beyond the usual, 'he's trying to buy my love' complaint that I've already told you is utter bullshit."

"I *was* mad at you. But the longer I thought about it, the more Kate seemed right. That I do have a right to the assistance fund, even if—" I catch myself before I blurt out the other really important news I need to tell Lauren. "So, I was mad at you for doing it behind my back. But I realize that I wouldn't have done it myself if you hadn't."

Lauren's crow of triumph is cut off by her choking on her mouthful of food. "Don't die, asshole."

I grin and push her my glass of water. "I admit you were right about it and I should have listened to you. But I'm still mad at Theo."

Getting her coughing under control, Lauren raises an eyebrow. "Why are you mad at Sutton? And please, for the love of the

Bluewater Billionaires, tell me why he's in such a fucking foul mood. He made Stuart *and* that new developer Frankie cry tonight."

The idea of that tall, patrician sack of male ego tearing up over something Theo said, has giggles bubbling up inside me, but from the exhaustion in Lauren's shoulders, it probably wasn't nearly as fun to live through as it is to think about after the fact. "She's so sweet, I hope you gave him a hard time for making her cry."

Lauren nods. "I saw him apologize later. So why are you mad at him?"

"He approved it. And I think he doubled it."

A spray of half-chewed chicken and rice lands in the middle of the counter at my announcement. "Doubled it?"

"It's the only thing I can think of. I went to talk to Kate. Um," I cough to cover my hesitation and hastily reach for the wine glasses I know Lauren keeps in the far-left cupboard, and snag the already open bottle I spotted in the fridge earlier. "Kate said that the amount was for thirty-thousand dollars, twice the normal limit of an application. And I didn't register the other things she said until later."

I pour us each a glass praying that Lauren doesn't call me out until I'm ready to tell her my other news. She takes the bait.

"What did she say?"

"That someone else submitted an internal application and doubled it. Who else besides Theo would know the exact amount of money Emma's hospital bill came to?"

Lauren sips from her glass, tapping it with her red-tipped nail. "I haven't told anyone else."

"Neither have I. And who else would be able to do something like that internally without tripping off some kind of alert?" We eat in silence for a few minutes. I don't know what's going through Lauren's head, but mine is whirling with how I'm going to tell her that I'm leaving Mailbox.

Finally, Lauren pushes her plate away and takes a long sip of her wine. "There's something else, isn't there, Soph?"

"What makes you say that?"

"Because you're a terrible actress and I can see the hamster running circles in your mind. I haven't known you for twenty years not to know when there's something on your mind. And it's not just about Sutton, is it?" She nudges my wine glass closer with her own. "Drink up and spit it out."

"You're a pushy bitch, you know that?" But I grab my glass and down the rest of the crisp white wine.

Lauren grins and pours us both another glass. "Yeah, but you love that about me. Besides, you're too nice to get rid of me at this point. Now spill."

"I was talking to Kate because I was giving my two weeks notice."

Dead silence is all I get in response.

I can't read the expression on her face. The silence drags on while Lauren calmly takes a long drink, the clink of her glass as she puts it back on the counter the only sound.

"I have two questions. One, do you have another job lined up?" She raises an eyebrow, indicating I should answer before she asks her next question. I nod. "Two, is this because of Sutton? Did he say or do something?"

I open my mouth to speak but Lauren interrupts me. "Wait, have you been looking for a new job and didn't tell me? Why didn't you tell me?"

I pause, waiting for another question but Lauren just crosses her arms and glares at me from across the kitchen island. Sighing, I push the last few grains of rice around on my plate while I speak, not meeting her eyes. "I started looking for a new job after the night we went out to that club. Remember how upset I was?" She nods. "It hit me hard that night that I couldn't keep going like I was and expect my life to change for the better. If I wanted my life to be better, then I needed to start making some changes. Starting with my job."

I glance up, expecting anger or confusion, not the sympathy I see in Lauren's eyes. Clearing my throat, I keep going. "I love Mailbox, but the truth is, I need to make more money. And yes, I probably could have looked for a position within the company. But I'm sure you and Theo would have noticed immediately and greased the wheels for me to make it happen. In fact, I *know* Theo would have done it. That's why I couldn't stay at Mailbox."

"You didn't want him to be the reason you got the job." Lauren's voice is soft. "I get that."

"It's one thing to have your best friend put in a good word for you. It's a whole different thing to have Portland's Most Eligible Bachelor tell his subordinates to give the receptionist the job."

"Especially if anyone found out he was sleeping with said receptionist."

"Exactly. Was he really awful?" I can't help asking. My heart twists at the idea of Theo being upset by my actions. I reach for her plate but she stops me, slapping my hand away.

"Stop that, I'll clean up. Worst I've ever seen. But he's a whole different issue and frankly, I'm over Theodore Sutton today. He can wait. I'm claiming best friend privilege and making this about me." She smirks and I laugh, pushing my worry about Theo aside. "I'm still kinda mad you didn't tell me you were looking for a new job. Ms. 'I play everything so close to the chest I don't tell my best friend important shit', but I get why you wanted to do it yourself. I've been telling you for months you need to make more money. What made you decide it was time?"

"You mean besides the hospital bill that was only a few thousand short of my annual salary?" Lauren snorts at that. "I'm sick of scraping by. Of sleeping on the goddamn couch because I can't afford a two-bedroom place, of not being able to buy my own goddamn drink at a bar. You and Theo kept offering to help me and I just...I just couldn't accept one more thing."

I take another long drink. "I've been so scared of failing, of leaving the safety of my job at Mailbox, it was the one thing that stayed the same when my life fell apart. I don't know, Lauren. The safety was starting to feel suffocating. I don't need to make millions, but I need to do more than just survive."

My best friend in the whole world grins at me. "Fucking finally!" At my confused snort, she clinks her wine glass to mine and salutes me with it. "I had given up hope that you were ever going to decide to do it. I love you more than anyone in the world, Soph, but you're a stubborn bitch when you want to be. I'm glad you finally figured it out. Money won't solve all your problems, but it sure makes dealing with them easier. Tell me about the new job. And do you know if you can keep writing as Elinor? 'Cause hiring another writer is going to be a pain in the ass."

Laughing, we take our glasses to the couch where Max is snoozing and I tell Lauren about the new company and my new job as a copywriter with them. For the first time in months, I relax and hang out with my favorite person, giggling and planning for my new job.

Lauren tells me about how she found the new girl crying in the bathroom. "I think we have to adopt her, Soph. She's only twenty-two and the dev bros are being real assholes to her. Fuck those guys. We're gonna turn her into a badass."

"I'm happy to adopt her, but if she's not a badass that's okay too. Invite her over on Friday—I'll cook."

We both avoid any mention of Theo. Lauren, because she's rightfully sick of talking about him with me. Me, because it hurts too much. I wish I could celebrate with him. I wish I knew he would be happy for me for doing this for myself. But that's wishful thinking on my part. How could he be happy for me? I'm leaving him.

I won't get to hide my smile at his scowly face every morning, knowing that he's faking it. Since he let me see inside his protective walls, I can tell he's hiding a smirk too. I see the way his hand twitches when he passes my desk, like he's fighting the urge to touch me. I don't know how I'm going to live without his gravelly voice saying, "Good morning Ms. Alexander," or the wink he drops when Julian isn't looking.

But I will.

I've survived before, I'll survive again. I have to.

Twenty-six

SOPHIE

SURVIVAL IS OVERRATED.

Surviving is also lonely as hell.

"Give it some time, you've only been at the new job for what, two weeks?" Lauren's question is hard to hear around her bite of salad and the noise of Uno, Dos, Tres, but I nod in agreement. "Pfft, you'll make friends in no time, Soph."

"I know. I don't know why I'm feeling this way, Lauren. I've been on my own for a year now. Nothing has changed except my job." I take a sip of water to clear my thoughts. When Lauren texted me last night to meet up for lunch today, I jumped at the chance. I miss seeing her and having lunch together. And even though I've only been at the new job for a couple of weeks, it feels like ages since we've had lunch together. Probably because my last two weeks at Mailbox I spent avoiding everyone as much as possible, and Lauren has been spending her lunches coaching Frankie on patriarchy-smashing.

But for the last month, loneliness has been eating away at me, especially at the end of a long day.

Lauren points at me with her fork. "I don't think you're lonely in general. I think you're lonely in particular." I wait for her to explain but she doesn't, stabbing her salad with the fork and taking a bite.

"What do you mean?" I finally ask after two more bites of her salad and my tacos pass in silence.

"I mean..." She waggles her eyebrows for emphasis. "You're lonely for one particular person. One Theodore-fuck-you-Sutton."

"I am not."

"You are too. Admit it, Soph. You miss him."

I lean back in my chair, arms crossed. "How can I miss something I never really had?"

"But you could have, if you'd been brave enough to try."

I flinch at Lauren's words. She's right and we both know it. Theo offered me everything—I was the one who was too scared to try, too scared to what might go wrong to find out what could go right.

"That ship has sailed." I scoop some fallen taco fillings up with a chip, stuffing it in my mouth to avoid the conversation. The savory carnitas and kick of lime on the cabbage and onion mix with the corn tortilla in my mouth, it tastes like perfection.

"Has it though? Have you even tried to talk to him again or are you hiding behind your excuses?"

I grimace. "I haven't spoken to him, but Emma won't stop talking about him."

"So you're just going to what? Be reminded of him all the time but never speak to him again? That doesn't exactly seem sustainable, Soph." Lauren shakes her head before taking a sip of her water.

"I just need time to find a new normal. Eventually I'll..." I trail off. I sound ridiculous, even to myself.

Lauren scoffs. "New normal? Sounds to me like you're resigning yourself to being unhappy. *Again*. You settled for the status quo with Jake and what did it ever get you?"

"A ton of debt and bad sex." My snarky answer gets a laugh from Lauren, but doesn't distract her from the point, unfortunately.

"You told me you wanted to take charge of your life, that you wanted to make the choices that were best for *you*. That's why you quit at Mailbox and got a new job, one that pays way more and doesn't have you fetching anyone's coffee, right? Is your job really the only thing in your life you weren't pursuing?"

She lets me stew over her words for a moment while she takes another bite of her lunch. I don't have a rebuttal because there isn't one. She's right. I wanted to make my life *mine*. Not in service to Jake's dreams or Emma's dreams. I want my life to be in service to me first, because if I don't put my own needs first to myself, who else would?

"I really fucking hate it when you're right, Lauren. It's annoying."

She laughs and I'm reminded how good a friend she is. Lauren is the only person in my life who has always encouraged me to take care of myself, even through the years when I couldn't see how much damage it was doing to my mental health. She could have washed her hands of me, but she's stuck by me through it all. "Okay, okay, I admit I'm chickening out when it comes to Theo. I just don't even know how to start that conversation. 'Oh hey, I'm sorry I was an asshole and rejected you every time you said you wanted to be with me. I know better now and I want to see you.'"

"I mean, maybe don't say it exactly like that, but that seems like a solid place to start."

"I'll think about it."

By the time we're done eating, the idea of talking to Theo again is fizzing in my veins. I've been ignoring the ache in my chest at the thought of him for weeks, chalking it up to regret rather than acknowledging the reality that I just plain miss him. I miss his gruff voice, his smirk, the leaps his brain takes when looking at a problem, the vulnerability I glimpsed in his eyes in those few precious moments we shared.

"Oh, I have something for Emma in my office, do you have time to come grab it?" Lauren hooks her arm through mine and starts walking the half block toward Mailbox's building.

A glance at my watch and I follow. "Yeah, I have some time. I don't have any meetings this afternoon, just some articles to edit. Did I tell you, last Friday everyone else in the office took two-hour lunches?"

Lauren laughs at the shock in my voice. "Don't laugh at me, I've never been on salary before, I didn't know that was a thing you could do, okay? It's weird being in a position where people trust me to just be a goddamn adult and get my work done."

I follow her into the lobby, stopping to say hello to Tina and Julian while Lauren gets the elevator. Hearing it ding behind me, I pull myself away from catching up with them and step inside with Lauren.

The doors close and we start moving up. "So what is it you have for Emma? Did she con you into buying that fancy ring light she's been wanting?"

"She conned all of us." Lauren grins as the elevator stops on the second floor and the doors open to reveal the man whose smile has been on my mind for months. "Hello, sir."

God, he looks good. His navy suit is perfectly tailored to his trim waist and sculpted shoulders. I have to stop myself from licking my lips at the memory of those arms caging me in against the windows in Seattle. His beard is trimmed short and neat, like always—his thick, dark hair swept back from his face. I want to run my fingers through it and mess it up. Just this glimpse of him and all my carefully suppressed longing for him roars to the surface, impossible to ignore.

"Ms. Masterson. Ms. Alexander, it's good to see you again."

Lauren scoots past me to exit the elevator and let Theo have it, as usual. I move to follow her, my face on fire, but he steps forward into the elevator car, blocking me. "Stay." When I hesitate, he rests a hand against my arm. "Please, Sunshine?"

As the elevator doors slide shut, I catch Lauren's grin and thumbs up over his shoulder. "Mr. Sutton—" I start to say, but he cuts me off with a growl. He hasn't stepped away and his scent, his presence, overwhelms me. I try to step back but his grip on my arm tightens a fraction before he steps even closer, his torso brushing my side. Releasing my arm, he reaches past me to the rows of buttons to my right. He flips open a small door, punching in a code.

"What are you doing?" I can't help asking. The floor numbers always used to light up in white, but now only the top floor button is illuminated in red.

"Making sure we don't get interrupted." His voice sends goosebumps down my spine. I should be worried—he's probably angry with me—but being trapped in the elevator with him, being near him, has me questioning how I ever walked away from him in the first place.

"How's the new job?"

Disappointment settles in my belly at the innocuous question. "Oh. It's good. Still getting used to it, but so far I like it."

His brows furrow and I want to run my fingers over them, ease the worry from his face. "Where is it again?"

A nervous laugh escapes me. "I'm over at Hype. I'm a junior copywriter and copyeditor. So far they mostly have me proofreading stuff other people have edited, but I'm enjoying it. My editor said she would start assigning me articles next week."

Theo nods, his eyes never leaving mine. Is he searching for something in my expression the same way I'm searching his? For some glimmer that he misses me, that I haven't ruined everything.

"So you're writing? That's great. I'm really happy for you, Sophie."

"I miss you." I blurt out before my brain can stop me. "God, I miss you so much."

For a second the silence in the elevator is deafening. My heartbeat pounds in my ears and I hold my breath, shocked at my confession. "Teddy, I'm so—"

My apology is swallowed by his searing kiss and Theo's arms pulling me flush against his body. Our tongues dance and his hands are everywhere but it's not enough, not close enough. My fingers wrap around the lapels of his jacket, pulling myself up on my toes as I pour everything into the fire between us.

With a groan, Theo backs me into the corner of the elevator. Sliding his hands down my sides, he cups my ass and lifts me up, pinning me against the wall with his hips. His already-hard cock teases me as he grinds his hips against me, while devouring my lips with his. "Fuck, Sunshine, I missed you too." He groans between kisses.

The clearing of a throat behind him startles a gasp from me and I pull back. Theo's assistant, Mercedes, stands in the open elevator doors, a knowing smirk on her face. "I see you're back early...from lunch."

Theo grins at me, a hint of the playful man I met outside these walls peeking through. "Mercedes, cancel the rest of my afternoon. And take a long lunch."

"Consider it done. Sophie, it's good to see you," Mercedes adds as Theo pulls me past her.

"Hi Mercedes, it's good to see you too!" I call over my shoulder as Theo drags me towards his office. "Teddy, slow down!" I laugh as I trip over my own feet, giggles escaping me. The fizzing in my veins from earlier has moved into my heart, Theo's hand in mine pushing away the loneliness that has been eating at me since I left Mailbox.

The floor is empty, since only Theo and Mercedes have offices up here, the conference rooms flanking his office abandoned on a Friday afternoon. Theo looks back over his shoulder at me, a predatory glint in his eye. My giggles die on my lips as his gaze drops to my breasts. "Sunshine..."

"Yes?"

"Say it again."

Neither of us look where we're going as we walk towards his office, the open door beckoning. "Say what?"

He drags me through the open door, spinning me past him to slam it shut and lock it. "Do you know how many times I have dreamed of this? Of having you here in my office?" He stalks toward me, unbuttoning his jacket and sliding it off his shoulders, I back up and he follows, dropping his jacket onto the chair next to me. My ass hits the edge of his desk and I squeak. There's nowhere to go, nowhere to hide from this man who has pursued me relentlessly, openly, with no pretense that he wants anything but me.

"Let me be absolutely clear, Ms. Alexander."

I shiver at the sound of my name on his lips.

"I never stopped missing you, or wanting you. Not seeing you every morning when I arrive, and every evening when I leave, has been agony. I've been an absolute terror around here since the day you quit, growling at everyone, simply because *you're* not here." He steps closer, dipping his head low to whisper in my ear, his lips tracing along my skin as he confesses. "But you, more than anyone, know that I only play the part of the asshole boss. My soft, squishy heart can't take it if you're not willing to do this for real. No pretense, no hiding."

Tears gather in my eyes as his words penetrate my stubborn heart. I can't speak, my mind and heart overwhelmed as he kisses along my neck and under my jaw. My hands grip the desk behind me, holding me up or anchoring me in place, I don't know.

He's not angry with me? After all the times I pushed him away—insisted I didn't want this, that I was fine without him—he can so easily tell me he still wants me, still wants us?

"How can you still want me? I was such a bitch to you." I croak out, my voice breaking on the last words.

"You were scared. Protecting yourself and Emma. If anyone understands about lashing out to protect yourself, it's me. I'd just never experienced it from the other side before you." His lips are warm and tender against my skin, contrasting with the rough stubble of his beard. One of his hands wraps around my waist, pulling us close. "And you were an asshole, not a bitch. You weren't trying to hurt me on purpose."

"But I did hurt you. And for that I'm sorry." I let go of the desk to run one hand against his cheek, burying my fingers in his hair. With a groan, Theo abandons my neck to bury his face between my breasts kissing and nipping at the swells, as I lightly stroke the soft strands beneath my palm.

"Apology accepted, but you haven't answered my question." His hands slide up my ribs to cup my breasts.

"Teddy..." His name is a sigh as his thumbs brush over my nipples, heat pooling in my core. Any resistance I had is gone, evaporated by the heat in his touch. "I don't work for you anymore."

"I'm aware." He abandons my breasts to look me in the eye.

I grip the knot of his tie and pull him close, our lips inches apart. "You're not my boss anymore. And I'm all in."

Like a firework exploding, our lips crash. His hands are everywhere at once, touching me, holding me, making sure this is real. My hands are desperate, pulling his tie loose before abandoning it to wrap my hands behind his neck. Theo pulls back with a gasp, grabbing my hands and pinning them to the desk behind me.

"Are you sure, Sunshine? Because I can't keep you a secret. I don't *want* to keep you a secret." His eyes search mine and I want to kick myself for putting that doubt there.

"I'm sure. I needed to prove to myself that I could do this on my own, that I could make a change and make my life and Emma's better. And I did." I squeeze the edge of the desk to stop myself from touching him.

"I would have helped."

"I know you would have, but I needed to do it for myself." I stop to take a shaky breath. "But I *could* have let you in and still done it. I kept telling myself that if I let you in, you'd take over and want to do everything for me and I didn't want that."

Theo grins. "I probably would have tried to help more than you wanted."

"You would have. And I would have resented it. But it doesn't matter now. What matters now is that I don't need rescuing anymore—but what I do need is *you*. I still want to say good morning to you every day, and good night every evening. Just not at work."

"I think that can be arranged. But first..." Theo steps close, pressing his hands down on the desk. "There's something I've been dying to do for longer than I care to admit." His eyes go dark with desire as he leans down to sip from my lips before kneeling in front of me. "Whatever happens, Ms. Alexander, do not let go of my desk."

My gasp is loud in the quiet office as Theo slides his hands up my thighs under my dress, his long fingers hooking over the edge of my underwear. "Shhhh. You wouldn't want them to hear you downstairs, Sunshine." He gives me a wicked grin before disappearing under the edge of my dress.

The warmth of his breath against my aching core is the only warning I get before his mouth devours me. Knees buckling, only my death grip on the edge of the desk keeps me from collapsing as he licks and sucks. "Oh God, Teddy."

"Mmmm, you taste better than I remembered." His voice is muffled, but the rumble against my clit is clear and oh so good. Theo's strong hands knead my ass as he pulls me closer, his tongue snaking inside my depths. My toes curl inside my shoes as an orgasm builds deep in my core.

His hands hold my hips steady against the desk as his thumbs slide against my lips, opening me up for another assault from his tongue. The scratch of his beard against the sensitive skin of my thighs paired with the new angle has stars exploding behind my eyes and my body collapsing entirely as the orgasm explodes through me.

Theo places a few tender kisses along the inside of my leg before he pushes to his feet. He leans down to kiss me, the taste of myself still on his lips sending another wave of heat through me.

"I have wanted to do that for so long," he whispers against my lips.

"Me too. Although, my fantasy involved the other side of the desk, truthfully." My giggle dies at the heat in Theo's gaze.

"Your fantasy?"

I nod, biting my bottom lip.

"Tell me more." His hard cock is pressed against my belly, making it difficult to think when I know just how good it feels inside me. "Ms. Alexander."

I gasp as his hard tone is accompanied by a rough hand sliding inside my dress to grab my ass.

"Am I, or am I not, the boss in this office?"

I nod, grinning when he rolls his hips against mine, rubbing that delicious length against me.

"In this office, but not of me." I counter, earning myself a hard nip to that perfect spot where neck and shoulder meet.

Theo's lips trail up my neck until he whispers in my ear. "If you don't tell me the fantasy, I can't make it come true. Let me make all your dreams come true."

Twenty-seven

THEO

SOPHIE GLANCES BEHIND HER at my desk, the files I was looking through before I got Lauren's text scattered across its surface. When she looks back at me, a wicked gleam in her eye, I steal another kiss at the same time I shove everything off onto the floor. "Is that what you want?" Her taste is still on my tongue.

My cock strains against my slacks, needing her, needing to be inside my Sunshine. The urge to claim her as mine is primal, but I hold back. Sophie bites her lip and nods before wrapping her arms around my neck and pulling me down on top of her as she lays back. God, if only she knew how many times I'd pictured the same scenario in the last two months.

Her hands slide down my chest to fumble with my belt buckle as I savor her lips and the way her tits push up out of her dress. I'd nearly swallowed my tongue at the sight of her in the elevator, despite knowing she would be there. The dark green dress nipped in at her waist before flaring out, the white cardigan in her hand evidence of the warm August afternoon.

I run my fingers over her cheek and into the blond locks strewn across my desk as she cups me through my pants. It's exquisite agony and I bite down on her neck in response.

"I need you, Teddy," she cries, squeezing my cock and wrapping her legs around the back of mine.

"I need you too, Sunshine. Hang on." I push myself up, not that I want to leave her, and circle around my desk to find what I'm looking for. Sophie sits up and swivels to face me, her legs swinging over the desk. "You're sure you're all in?" I turn to ask, the condom I'd fished out from the back of my desk drawer in hand. "Because there are so many things I want to do to you right now—I need to know I'll get to have you in my office again or I might explode from trying to do everything at once."

Sophie's musical laugh fills the quiet. "I'm in, Teddy. For as long as you are."

"You promise not to run away again?" I didn't mean to say it, but my racing heart and the giddiness from having Sophie back in my arms has gone straight to my head, bypassing every shield and filter I've put in place over the years. Her eyes go wide for a second, before she reaches up to cup my cheek.

"For as long as you are," she repeats softly.

Heart still hammering, I lean down to take her lips with mine. I trace her face with my fingers as she unzips my pants, plucking the condom from the desk where I left it. "Let's just start with today," she whispers.

I slide into her, arms wrapped behind her back as we move in rhythm together. As cliché as it is, having sex in the boss's office, it also feels right, like home. Being with Sophie is a comfort so deep in my bones that I'm in no rush to finish. I want to savor the moment, trusting that no one will disturb us, at least not yet.

I bury myself in her, sliding my cock in and out of her almost languidly as I kiss her. "I wasn't sure I'd ever get you back." I reach down to pull her hips to the edge of the desk.

"I didn't think you'd still want me." Sophie's arms around my neck pull me close. "Oh yes," she cries out as I slip a finger between us, circling her clit. At her cry, the urge to just take her, to claim her, roars to the surface and I can't hold back any longer.

One of her legs wraps behind my ass, the heel of her shoe digging in and pulling me closer. I slam into her with more force than before, picking up the pace. "You like that, Soph? Do you like being fucked in my office? On my desk?"

At my rough words, Sophie pulls back, grinning. "Yes, I do, Mr. Sutton." She winks and grabs the front of my shirt, quickly undoing the top buttons. "Theodore-fuck-me-Sutton...is that the best you can do?"

With a grunt, I pick up the pace, slamming my cock into this woman who's claimed me body and soul, my thumb still circling her clit. Her cries and my groans meld into each other, filling the office along with the heavy scent of sex. Another orgasm ripples through Sophie, the walls of her core milking mine from me. I come with a roar I muffle only by kissing her hard.

Spent, I lean one hand down on the desk behind her, my head buried in her neck. I don't want to be separated from her yet, not when I can feel the golden light of my Sunshine piecing me back together again. Sophie's fingers trail up and down my spine, the fabric of my shirt sticking to me in the heat. I'm in a daze, but the shaking of her shoulders snaps me out of it.

"Are you—?" I was about to say crying, but the grin on her face tells me everything I need to know. I ease myself out of her and get rid of the condom, tying it off and dumping it in the trash can beneath my desk. "What's so funny?"

Sophie kicks her feet, still giggling. "It's just...we never did this while I was actually working here, even though we'd both imagined it so many times. It wouldn't be the same if we got caught now."

I tuck my shirt back in and zip up my pants. "Maybe not, but it would still be a scandal." I wink as I re-button my shirt.

"It would." Sophie grins. "Oh shit, I should go. I have to get back to work. I wouldn't want my new boss to get mad at me." She hops off the edge of my desk, straightening her dress and running her fingers through her hair. "Where's my...?"

I hold up her lace underwear, "Nope, these are mine now."

"Theo! I can't go back to work without—"

I cut her off with another kiss. "You can. I'm not giving them back until I see you again." Am I playing dirty to make sure Sophie doesn't change her mind? Absolutely.

"Fine. I'll text you later, I have to go." She turns to rush out the door but I pull her back for one more kiss. "Oh! Lauren said she had something to give me, I should—."

"Me. She brought you back here for me."

"She did?"

I nod, kissing her one more time. "She did. Now go, before I decide to kidnap you for the rest of the afternoon."

I follow her to the elevator, kissing her long and sweet while we wait for the doors to open. Pulling back, I drop my forehead to Sophie's, afraid if I let her go she'll disappear again. "I'll see you later?"

The doors open with a ding, Mercedes inside. Sophie glances sideways, then presses a quick kiss to my lips. "I'll see you later. I promise."

Mercedes says nothing while Sophie steps inside and the doors close. "Well, that was easier than I expected."

"What do you mean?" I run a hand through my hair, settling it back in place.

"I thought she'd be more stubborn than that—maybe she's smarter than I gave her credit for." She follows me as I trudge back to my desk. "I assume you're going to work from home this afternoon. After you've, ahem, cleaned up here?"

Heat creeps up the back of my neck as I survey the mess left in my office. Papers are scattered across the floor, along with some pens and my rubber duck from MIT. "Uh, yeah. Thank you, Mercedes."

She laughs as she settles herself at her desk. "My lips are sealed. I just hope she makes you happy."

"She does, Mercedes. She does."

Emma and Sophie's voices carry down the stairs as I take them two at a time. I don't think they're arguing, but I can't tell from this distance.

"—I didn't, Mom. I promise."

"Emma, you know we can't afford it. Give me the login so I can cancel it."

"Mom, I swear, there's nothing to cancel."

There's a large box on the doorstep. Swallowing hard, I speak up before Emma takes the blame. "Knock, knock." I peek my head inside the door to find Sophie and Emma standing nose to nose in front of the couch.

"Theo!" Sophie jumps back, looking around. "I didn't expect you so soon. I, uh, haven't, umm..."

I have to work to keep my face under control. She's so adorable when she's flustered.

"Teddy, tell my mom I didn't order that." Emma points to the box at my feet without acknowledging her mom's discomfort.

I pick up the box, the branding on it proudly proclaiming its origin from a high-end ready-made meal kit company. "This one? Why? What's wrong with it?"

Sophie huffs. "I didn't order it. We *talked* about trying one once school started, but we also talked about waiting until the paychecks from my new job started coming in."

"Mom, I didn't order it."

Sophie opens her mouth to say something but I cut her off. "I did."

Sophie swivels to face me, mouth hanging open. "You? But..."

I carry the box into the apartment, setting it on their tiny table. "I did."

"But...why?" Sophie hands me a pair of scissors and I slice the top open.

I take a second to survey the contents before I answer. "Because Sunshine, I wanted to make your life easier. I know you can buy groceries yourself, and I know you can cook, but this saves you a trip to the store. And I know you'll be getting high quality ingredients, because I know you, you'll buy all the no-name brands and cheapest things."

"But, Theo. You had to have ordered this days ago." Sophie is still standing in her kitchen, scissors in hand, looking for all the world like I just told her that pickles taste like candy. "We only just…"

"I helped." Emma pipes up, coming to help put away the contents of the box. "Teddy was cooking when I brought Max home the other day and—"

"Wait, what do you mean when you brought Max home? What is going on?"

I glance at Emma and she shoos me out of the kitchen space. "I got this, you better go sort it out."

Taking Sophie by the hand, I pull her away from the kitchen to sit on the couch. She sinks down next to me, arms crossed, and waits. "Well, see." Now that I'm having to explain the situation it sounds so much worse than it seemed at the time. "I came home from work one day and Emma was at my house, waiting for me."

"You went to his house!" Sophie starts to get up but I put a hand on her leg, stopping her.

"She wanted me to hire her to walk Max a couple of days a week. So she could earn some money without having to ask you for it." The look of mistrust hasn't left Sophie's face yet, but she doesn't interrupt, nor does she look like she's about to throttle Emma, so I continue. "I didn't want to hire her. In fact, I was pretty awful about it."

"Yeah, you were a real asshole at first." Emma calls from the kitchen.

"Emma! Language!" Sophie's cheeks turn bright pink at Emma's swearing. "I'm sorry—"

"It's fine. Emma's a good kid. And I should be the one apologizing. I was an asshole to your daughter, but she caught me on a bad day."

"What day was it?"

"The day you gave notice."

"Oh."

"Yeah. But after refusing to hire her to be my dog-walker, I offered to give her a ride home so she didn't have to walk all that way." I rub a hand on the back of my neck, still regretting how I handled myself that day. "Anyway, we got talking in the car and Emma mentioned that you were still struggling with the bills, and I mentioned how you wouldn't let anyone help you."

I talk faster to stop Sophie from interjecting. "We started brainstorming ways I could maybe make your life a little easier, without you knowing it."

"The GrubHub gift card that she 'won'?"

"It counts. I 'won' it from Teddy in a game of Uno." Emma calls from her hiding place in the kitchen.

I grin. "She won it from me fair and square."

"The spending money that Lauren gave you?" Sophie glares through the wall to the kitchen.

"That actually was from Lauren. But Teddy also paid me for walking Max that day."

"So you really have been walking his dog?" Sophie glares at me now.

I rub my beard to hide my smile. "She's been an excellent employee."

"What about the manicure-pedicure certificate that Lauren just happened to have?" Sophie asks, examining her bright pink nails.

"I decided that *all* of the freelance writing staff deserved a treat." I shrug. Lauren hadn't been hard to win over, once she knew I was serious.

"Have you all been in...?" Sophie struggles for a word. I wait, watching her face change as she works out the tiny ways I've been smoothing her path over the last few weeks. "The free Starbucks? But that wasn't your car in front of me..."

"I was three cars ahead. I paid for all of the cars between us as well." I shrug, Emma had been texting me her and Sophie's locations whenever they went out and I'd managed to find ways of being there.

"You're telling me you've been in...been in *cahoots* with Emma and Lauren this whole time and I had no idea?" Sophie hops to her feet, pacing back and forth in front of me. "Okay, but this." She waves towards the kitchen. "This is too much, Teddy. You couldn't have known that today would happen."

Out of the corner of my eye, Emma sneaks into her room, making a show of putting in her earbuds as she goes. I smile. She's a good kid. And she's been surprisingly fun to hang out with when she brings Max home from his walks. The slobbery mutt is besotted with her.

I grab Sophie's hand and pull her down next to me. Taking her by the hands, I look into those bright blue eyes I adore so much. "I didn't know, you're right. That wasn't the point. I was prepared to do this for as long as it took for you to let down your guard and let me back in."

A strand of her corn silk hair falls in front of her eyes and I reach up to smooth it back. "All I want is to make your life better, Sunshine. No, what I *need* is to know that your life is good. Whether or not I'm in it, I want you to be able to enjoy it. To have the comfort of an ice-cold coffee on a scorching Saturday afternoon, or a nice meal cooked at home after a long day at work."

Her eyes go glassy, but there's a tiny smile creeping around the edges of her mouth, so I keep talking. "I know you could do this on your own. Nothing I've done is taking that away from you, Sunshine. I just want to be part of it—that's all I'm asking. Let me in. Let me be part of your life."

"Didn't we already discuss this?" There's a teasing note to her voice. "What did I tell you earlier?"

"That you were in it with me." Now there's tears in my own eyes. The broken pieces of my heart fuse together in the light of her smile.

"Are you really? You didn't spend the afternoon at work talking yourself out of it?"

"I didn't and I am. For as long as you're in it."

I reach over and pull Sophie onto my lap, letting the weight of her ground me in this moment. "And if I say forever?"

Sophie sighs, her breath dancing along my lips as she leans close. "Then forever it is."

I pull her close, needing her sweetness and light, pressing my lips to hers in an unspoken promise to be everything she needs and more, just like she is for me.

The click of Emma's bedroom door opening and closing again has me cracking one eye open. "Ugh, gross. This is what I'm going to have to live with now?"

Sophie explodes into giggles, ducking her head into my chest. I throw my head back and laugh with her, the usual weight of being Theodore Sutton floating away on the wings of her laughter. Emma stands by the door watching us, head cocked. "Bella's on her way over. Are you guys going to stay here and be gross, or what?"

I help Sophie off my lap then stand up beside her. "Nope, I'm taking your mom out for dinner. You can order whatever you want to eat, my treat." I pull out my phone to tap a few buttons before nodding to my pint-sized partner in crime.

"Don't keep her out too late." Emma winks at me before giving her mom a hug. "Now go away, I can't stomach your..." she waves her hand at the pair of us. "This."

I reach out to flip her hair. "You better get used to it, you're stuck with me now."

Sophie is watching the pair of us, an amused expression on her face. "Are you two done?"

I nod, squeezing her into my side.

"Be good and don't be obnoxious. We won't be out too late. Love you." Sophie pulls Emma in to kiss the top of her head before I drag her out the door.

We're halfway down the stairs when Emma calls out from above us. "Love you too! Don't come home too early, I'm having a raging party while you're gone!"

Epilogue

THE PILE OF BOXES sitting in Teddy's doorway is pitiful, really. The old me would have been mortified that the contents of mine and Emma's lives could be contained in so few boxes, but the old me also would have argued longer with Teddy when he asked us to move into his house.

A year ago, after we'd been dating for a few months and the lease was up on the minuscule place Emma and I had been living in, I was still too afraid of things falling apart to take him up on his offer to move in together. With my new job at Hype, I'd been able to afford to move us into a much nicer, and bigger, two-bedroom house, and my pride had dictated that I do that, rather than move in with Teddy right away.

But when it had come time to renew that lease, Teddy and Emma had teamed up to point out the myriad ways our lives would be better if I would just accept the inevitable. I'm trying not to think too hard about Emma's final point—that she was going away to college next year and she didn't want me to be all alone in the house. Teddy had done his convincing in private. He was very persuasive.

"Hey, Sunshine." Teddy's lips tickle the back of my ear as his arms circle my waist. "Is that the last of them?"

I lean back against him, letting him support me. I've been practicing, letting Teddy support me as much as I support him. It took me a while, and more than a few arguments to get used to the fact I didn't actually have to ask him to help me. He just quietly notices where he can make my life easier and does it. "Yup. Emma's stuff is already in her room. This is mostly books, I think."

"Good. Come out to the backyard—this can wait." He tugs me through the house, toward the voices I hear out there. I'm sweaty and tired, my clothes smudged with dirt and my hair knotted up on top of my head. All I really want is to use the amazing shower in Teddy's, no, our, bathroom.

"But—"

"No buts, we have guests, you know." He grins over his shoulder at me and I stop arguing. He's up to something, but I don't want to ruin his fun, even if I am exhausted.

"Do family count as guests? Can I at least shower?"

"They do when they fly in from LA for our housewarming."

"Is it a housewarming party if you've lived here for six years already?" I smile as we have the same argument as two days ago, when Teddy informed me his sister and her family were coming to visit the day Emma and I were moving in.

He doesn't answer me, just pulls me through the French doors into the backyard. Garrett is already grilling while Emma and Frankie play with Ethan and Clara out on the grass, Max barking and dancing at their heels. Lauren is chatting easily with Casey, a sharp contrast to the first time she'd met Teddy's famous sister and husband.

I think we were all a little star-struck the first time we'd met them. Frankie in particular—she isn't nearly as timid now as she was when Lauren and I first introduced her to Casey and Garrett. She's become a regular staple in our little squad, Emma's adopted her as a sort of big sister.

"Sophie!" Garrett, sets his tongs down and picks me up in a bear hug, my feet swinging uselessly beneath me. "You look fucking fantastic as always!"

Laughing, I squirm until Garrett puts me down. "Yeah, right. I'm disgusting, but thanks Garrett. Are your muscles even bigger than last time I saw you?"

Casey laughs, pushing Garrett out of the way to give me a hug. "He wishes." She adds in my ear, "He's got a complex because Chris Hemsworth got the 'muscles of the decade' award by some magazine last month. He's been working out twice a day ever since—it's awful."

Teddy rescues me with a grin, pulling me into his side. "How come you were out here with the grill while the movers and I were sweating it out with all those boxes, huh?"

"Oh, you know. Didn't want to draw a crowd." Garrett winks and my cheeks go pink in response. He may be Teddy's brother-in-law, but no one with a uterus is immune to the effect of that face, not even me.

"Have you shown her yet?" Lauren comes to my rescue, calling out from the lawn chair she's draped over.

"Not yet, give me a minute." Teddy grumbles. Why is he all grumbly and growly?

I slide my hand down to twine my fingers with his. "Show me what? Can I see it now?"

"No time for that, burgers are ready." Garrett flourishes his tongs. "Kids! Food!"

Hours later I'm full of food and falling asleep in Teddy's lap as he jokes with Casey about some prank they pulled on Garrett when they were kids. "Hey," Teddy wakes me up with a kiss to the side of my head. The sun is setting and the late-summer air is crisp, the dried sweat on my body chilled in the night air. "You okay?"

"I'm exhausted. But happy." I snuggle back into his lap, seeking the warmth of his body.

"Yeah?"

I nod sleepily against him, but don't answer. "Hey, I have something to show you."

The reminder of Lauren's earlier question has my brain perking up a little. "Right now?"

Teddy pushes to his feet, picking me up and setting me on mine before he takes my hand. I follow him in a tired daze to the room he designated for my office, one that adjoins his with an open doorway so Max can lay in the middle and keep an eye on both of us. There's a brand-new desk by the window, my laptop and writing notes already set up. A squashy-looking easy chair is in the corner, a throw rug and ottoman completing a cozy reading nook. I can tell Casey and Lauren must have been busy in here because the décor is perfectly me, only nicer than I would have picked out for myself. "Is this for me?"

"Yup. Everything you need is in here." Teddy gives me a gentle push into the room. Bookshelves line one wall, one of them already filled with familiar looking paperbacks.

"How did you—?" All the books my author friends have published in the last few years are there. The ones I wanted to buy in paperback and didn't because I didn't have the space, or money, for it. Not only are all my friends books here, but my favorite authors too. I run my fingers across the tops, sniffing at the books. "When did you do all this?"

Teddy runs a hand through his hair, glancing around. "Lauren helped. She got in touch with all the authors I didn't know about, and got them to send their books." He steps closer, reaching out to tuck an escaped strand of hair back into my messy bun. "I wanted you to have a space where you could pursue your dream. I know you love your job at Hype, but when you're ready to pursue your writing for real, and that's entirely up to you Sunshine, I wanted you to have everything you could need to make it happen."

I rise up on my toes to press a kiss to his lips. "I love you."

He kisses me back for a long moment. "I love you too. That's not all, look inside."

"Inside the books?" I ask, not sure where this is going. "What more can there be, you gave me a library office, it's every bookworm's dream in here." I wave my hands at the floor to ceiling shelves lining the wall. He just smiles and nods towards the shelf.

I pull down a random book and flip it open to the title page.

"*Say yes. Love, Alina*" is inscribed inside it. Weird—that's not what Alina usually writes in her books.

I pull down another one. "*Say yes bisch. Love, Las.*"

I pull down more and more books, they all say the same thing. "Say yes."

There's even one from Nora-freaking-Roberts with the same inscription. Tears are already running down my cheeks by the time I stop pulling out books and turn to find Teddy behind me. He's not on one knee like I expected, but he is grinning down at me.

"I figured I'd give you time to get used to the idea before I did it officially, in case you got stubborn about it. But just know..." He looks toward the doorway. I follow his glance to see Emma, Casey, Lauren and Garrett grinning at us. "Emma gave me her blessing and we went shopping for rings the other day. I'm ready whenever you are, just say the word, boss."

"Yeah?"

"That would be the one I'm hoping for, yeah."

I slide my hands down his arms to twine my fingers with his. "Yes."

Teddy stares down at me for a second, his eyes glassy. "You mean it? That's it? You're in, just like that?"

"I'm in for as long as you are, remember?" I whisper, giving him a watery smile.

"Forever?"

"Forever."

Can't get enough of the Mailbox, Inc crew?

Preorder Chief-of-Security now!

Sign up for my newsletter to receive your
free copy of Casey and Garrett's story
https://www.subscribepage.com/fancyrobertsnewsletter

Acknowledgments

Thanks to my real-life Lauren. She'll never read this book but she's on every page. When I write Lauren's story, you better believe I'm writing the HEA I would give to her—my platonic life partner who's been a better spouse to me and co-parent to my kiddo than my ex-husband ever was.

The reason this book even exists is because of Lasairiona McMaster. If she hadn't needed one more story for her Good Vibes anthology, I wouldn't have committed to finishing this. I hate-love you bish.

I started writing this book at one a.m. after being woken from a dead sleep by my now ex-husband. The reason doesn't matter any more, but nothing gets a good story going like sleep-deprived rage. You can thank my real-life Jake for this. Although I have yet to find myself a Theo. If you know a good one send him my way, okay?

And thank you, reader, for taking a chance on this book and me.

About Author

Fancy Roberts likes her heroes how she likes her coffee—hot, strong, and at least twice a day. Classy on the outside, and sassy on the inside, Fancy loves nothing more than to drop a well-timed profanity and tell a sexy story.

Just like her, Fancy's heroines are more than meets the eye and give as good as they get. The road to their happily ever after may be rocky, but she promises everyone gets what they deserve in the end.

Besides, who doesn't love a woman who orders a whiskey, neat, then tells you a dirty joke while wearing a twinset and pearls?